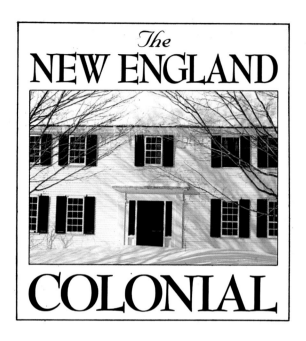

The NEW ENGLAND

COLONIAL

AMERICAN DESIGN

The
NEW ENGLAND

COLONIAL

TEXT BY ANNE ELIZABETH POWELL
PHOTOGRAPHS BY JOE VIESTI
FOREWORD BY J. JACKSON WALTER,
PRESIDENT, THE NATIONAL TRUST FOR HISTORIC PRESERVATION
INTRODUCTION BY VIRGINIA AND LEE McALESTER
DESIGN BY JUSTINE STRASBERG AND B. W. HONEYCUTT
Produced by The Miller Press, Inc. and IMG Publishing

BANTAM BOOKS · TORONTO · NEW YORK · LONDON · SYDNEY · AUCKLAND

To the memory of my father,
Arthur Gorman Powell, Jr.,
who pointed me in the right direction
and gave me the grit and courage
I needed to make the journey.

—ANNE ELIZABETH POWELL

To my wife Diane, whose patience
and understanding made this work
possible.

—JOE VIESTI

THE NEW ENGLAND COLONIAL
A Bantam Book / October 1988

LIBRARY OF CONGRESS
Library of Congress Cataloging-in-Publication Data

Powell, Anne Elizabeth.
The New England Colonial / text by Anne Elizabeth Powell;
photographs by Joe Viesti;
foreword by J. Jackson Walter; introduction by Virginia
and Lee McAlester.
p.   cm. —(American design)
Bibliography: p. 247
ISBN 0-553-05310-8
1. Architecture, Domestic—New England.   2. Architecture,
Colonial—New England.   I. Title.   II. Series.
NA7210.P68 1988
728.3'7'0974—dc19   88-14036   CIP

Published simultaneously in the United States and Canada

Bantam Books are published by Bantam Books, a division of Bantam
Doubleday Dell Publishing Group, Inc. Its trademark, consisting of the
words "Bantam Books" and the portrayal of a rooster, is Registered in U.S.
Patent and Trademark Office and in other countries. Marca Registrada.
Bantam Books, 666 Fifth Avenue, New York, New York 10103.

Printed in Italy by New InterLitho S.p.A. - Milan

0 9 8 7 6 5 4 3 2 1

ACKNOWLEDGMENTS

While the legacy of the New England colonists is considerable, there is perhaps no greater testimony to their strength, their mettle, and their spirited resolve to make their way in a new land than the dwellings they built, a fair number of which stand proudly yet today. The continued survival of these houses is dependent, of course, upon the thoughtful and diligent care of owners who take as much pride in the structures as did their builders. Those who nurture these venerable houses are a special breed indeed and to the following among them who so generously offered *their* New England colonials for inclusion in this book, I offer my warmest thanks for their generosity and hospitality: Richard and Wendy Anderson, Margaretta Clulow, Howard and Dorothy Crockett, Serge and Patty Gagarin, Ken and Barbara Hammitt, James and Alice Houston, Mary Louise Meyer, the Honorable and Mrs. Endicott Peabody, Steve and Kitty Petty, Chuck and Pat Pope, Jim and Audrey Simon, Bruce and Mary Sterne, Dudley and Sally Willis, and the several who wish to remain unnamed.

I would also like to extend my gratitude to: all of those who helped to shape this book, especially Angela Miller, Jennie McGregor, and Carla Glasser of IMG Publishing and Coleen O'Shea, Becky Cabaza, and Lucy Salvino of Bantam Books for their patience, understanding, and guidance; and Joe Viesti for the meticulous care he took in producing the superb photography and for the marvelous sense of humor he injected into many a long day. On behalf of IMG Publishing, I would like to thank Chippy Irvine, Margaret Luchans of the Cooper Hewitt Museum library, Virginia McAlester, Carl Nelson, Tina Strasberg and B.W. Honeycutt, Ken Hurley of Adroit Graphic, and Nan Jernigan.

Thanks also to those whose insights and suggestions helped me with the research, particularly David Howard, Lydia Kinmonth, Peter English, Edward Winston-Sykes, and James Dennison; and to some special people who helped in special ways—my mother, Barbara Powell, who offered her wisdom at the outset and her encouragement throughout; John Ebeling, who believed in me long before I believed in myself and whose continued love and support mean so much; my sister, Holly Puglisi, from whom I gained a new perspective; Eric Heintz, who helped me slay the dragon that had long blocked my path; Estelle Bond Guralnick, who, as always, came through with an absolute gem in a hurry; Patricia McCarthy of *Mid-Atlantic County* magazine, who understood the importance of this project and generously assumed my responsibilities during my absences; and last, but certainly not least, Bob Dittmer and Pam Wilson, whose friendships are golden and who helped me more than they know.

ANNE ELIZABETH POWELL

CONTENTS

Massachusetts

4

CHESTNUT BROOK FARM   12
A Simple 1703 Saltbox in Sherborn

MARY BALLANTYNE
ASHLEY HOUSE   24
*A 1738 Saltbox in the Berkshire
Mountains*

CHARLESCOTE FARM   36
*A 1759 Georgian Estate Outside
of Boston*

Connecticut

46

JOHN BANKS HOUSE   54
*A 1739 Wood-Shingle Farmhouse
in Fairfield*

SABBATH DAY HOUSE   68
*A Converted 1740 Meeting House
in Woodbury*

THOMAS BUCKINGHAM
HOUSE   80
*A Contemporary Renovation of
a 1785 Maritime House in Essex*

CAPTAIN AMOS PALMER
HOUSE   94
*A Privateer's Elegant 1787
Town House in Stonington*

Rhode Island

106

JOSEPH REYNOLDS
HOUSE   114
*A Three-Story 1695 Red
Clapboard in Bristol*

VERNON HOUSE   126
*A 1758 High-Style Georgian
Town House in Newport*

ISAAC PECK HOUSE   138
*An 1809 Two-Family House
Reconfigured in Providence*

Maine

148

THOMAS PERKINS
HOUSE   156
*A 1724 Saltbox on the Banks
of the Kennebunk River*

FARNSWORTH   170
*A 1760 Center-Chimney House
in Waldoboro*

Vermont

182

ELIJAH WRIGHT HOUSE   188
*A 1792 Farmhouse Near
Lake Champlain*

RECONSTRUCTED
COLONIAL   200
*A 1680 Saltbox and an 1840
General Store Joined in
Windsor County*

New Hampshire

214

MATTHEW HARVEY
HOUSE   220
*A 1784 White Clapboard Near
the Sunapee Mountains*

PARSONAGE   234
*A Stately 1811 Wood and Brick
Federal House in Hollis*

FOREWORD   viii
INTRODUCTION   2
SOURCE LIST   242
BIBLIOGRAPHY   247

FOREWORD

hen urban renewal reached its heyday in the 1950s and 1960s, when hundreds of American cities were bulldozing their old downtown commercial and residential neighborhoods, one of New England's premier preservationists, Antoinette F. Downing, stepped to the fore. She wrangled a federal grant for what was perhaps the earliest use of city planning funds for preservation. Numerous hearings and public discussions led to publication in 1959 of the *College Hill Study*, which strongly recommended preservation as an integral part of Providence's public policy. As a result, Providence harbors one of the nation's largest intact troves of eighteenth- and nineteenth-century architecture, and serves as a model for similar efforts throughout New England.

Antoinette Downing is a devout restoration advocate who almost never touches a paintbrush, an academic in a mostly blue collar community, an outsider in a small city where everyone you meet is a native, and a volunteer appointee who reports to work everyday in a field increasingly dominated by professionals. She has been an ardent preservationist for fifty-six years and, at eighty-three, is every bit as active today as she was in the 1950s.

Her efforts should inspire anyone with a concern for protecting the architectural heritage of early American settlers. She has spent most of her life in the tireless pursuit of one goal: to make the citizens of Rhode Island appreciate their historic buildings. She is a founding member of the Providence Preservation Society and has served on the group's executive board since 1956. In 1968, she was the first and since then has been the only chairman of the Rhode Island Historical Preservation Commission, and since 1960 she has been the only chairman of the Providence Historic District Commission.

Moreover, her influence extends far beyond the borders of America's smallest state. Antoinette Downing advises preservation groups from Colonial Williamsburg to Ann Arbor, Michigan. She served as an advisor and trustee of the National Trust for Historic Preservation throughout the 1970s and into the 1980s. She has been honored by everyone from the American Institute of Architects to the U.S. Department of the Interior. In 1987 she received the preservation movement's highest honor, the Louise du Pont Crowninshield Award, from the National Trust. In the late 1940s, the then brand new Preservation Society of Newport County asked her to survey Newport's historic houses. In 1952 she and the young scholar Vincent Scully produced *The Architectural Heritage of Newport, Rhode Island*. It was a new type of book: not only a history but a plan of action to preserve these places. This work helped save the great summer homes of the Gilded Age and Newport's 400 colonial houses; one of them was the Vernon House featured in this book, for which Antoinette Downing consulted on the restoration.

Antoinette Downing always has been in the forefront of preservation. As a scholar, she published *Early Homes of Rhode Island* in 1937, helping stimulate the beginnings of the now widespread interest Americans have in their colonial heritage.

The New England Colonial continues in this tradition. Because of good care, and the remarkable dedication of preservationists such as Antoinette Downing, and the Society for the Preservation of New England Antiquities, hundreds of New England colonial houses have survived. These houses are functional, beautiful, and remarkable places to live in. And they are an irreplaceable part of America's architectural heritage.

J. JACKSON WALTER
*President
National Trust
for Historic Preservation*

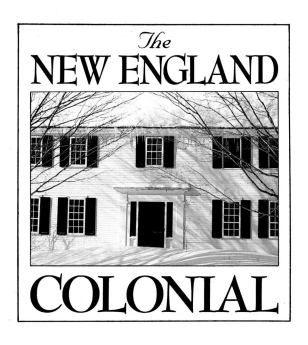

The
NEW ENGLAND
COLONIAL

INTRODUCTION

No house type is more deeply ingrained into our nation's collective memory than the New England Colonial. A variety of different housing traditions dominated the other American colonies of the same era—Southern English, Spanish, French, and Dutch —yet it is the dwellings of colonial New England that have come to symbolize our country's origins and democratic ideals. This book provides a delightful sampling of sixteen of these most familiar of all American houses.

The earliest New England colonists built copies of the simple Medieval houses that still dominated the rural England they had just left behind. Only a few of these houses from the 1600s have survived to the present day in anything like their original appearance. Most were updated and reconfigured during the 1700s, when the Georgian and Federal styles came into fashion, or received even more drastic updating in later decades. Hallmarks of these first houses as they were originally constructed were steeply pitched roofs (a holdover from thatched roof coverings, which must be steeply inclined to shed water), small window panes (larger pieces of glass were not yet economical to produce), and huge chimneys, usually centered in New England houses to serve fireplaces in every room and to minimize heat loss.

The chimney itself was then a novel innovation, having become common in England only shortly before the first colonists left for the New World. Previously, most houses had open central fires and no ceilings— smoke simply rose to the high roof peak and escaped through small side-openings. The far more efficient heating properties of fireplaces with chimneys proved to be literal lifesavers during the bitterly cold New England winters.

Steep roofs framed with heavy timbers limited most of these early houses to one-room depths, for deeper spans were very complex and expensive to construct. The most common plan was two stories high with two adjacent rooms on each floor. Later the familiar *saltbox* shape was developed as a simple means of extending the steep roofs to cover two additional rear rooms on the first floor. By the early decades of the 1700s, innovations in roof framing made it possible to span a two-room depth, leading to *massed plan* houses with symmetrical roof lines and a full four rooms on each floor. These quickly became common throughout New England, where the long and snowy winters restricted outdoor activities and made large houses, as well as attached barns and other dependencies, particularly desirable.

During these same decades a new fashion in architectural decoration—the Georgian style—was sweeping New England. Georgian houses are direct descendants of the artistic Renaissance that had begun in Italy two centuries earlier. Stylistic innovations traveled slowly in those days, and the stately Georgian facades of New England that we so admire today had a particularly long journey. From fifteenth-century Italy they gradually spread northward into France, from which they ultimately crossed the Channel into remote England. There, Renaissance-based designs began to replace Medieval buildings in the mid-1600s. It then took another fifty years before the Renaissance finally crossed the Atlantic to become the dominant "Georgian" fashion in England's newly prosperous American colonies.

Hallmarks of Renaissance-inspired houses are symmetrical window balance and classical details applied to an otherwise flat facade. In New England, the doorway and the cornice line beneath the roof became the primary sites of decorative elaboration in all but the very largest and most pretentious examples. The cornice usually sported toothlike dentils, and the door had flattened columns on either side that supported a more or less elaborated crown, or entablature, above. Commonly a single line of lights (small window panes) was also added over the solid door to provide light to the entry area.

Windows of uniform size and placement complemented the decorative central doorway, creating a harmoniously balanced facade. The details of window design changed as glassmaking techniques improved during the 1700s. The small square panes—eight, nine, or even twelve per window sash—that occurred early in the century were almost completely replaced by the closing decades with larger panes that required only six pieces to fill each sash.

The final stylistic era of the New England Colonial is the Federal style, which is a more refined version of the preceding Georgian style. The Federal style became popular in England and the United States in the last decades of the 1700s. This is not strictly a "colonial" style, as it did not become popular until after the American Revolution. It was, nonetheless, borrowed from England and evolved from the earlier Georgian so that it is most logically grouped with the preceding colonial styles. In England the style was popularized by the fashionable architects Robert Adam and his three brothers; there it is known as the Adam style. In deference to our country's newly-won independence, it is usually referred to here as the Federal style.

The Federal house differed only slightly from the preceding Georgian, to which it added a new lightness and delicacy. Windows, both the total opening and the individual panes, became larger and more finely detailed. Curved-top fanlights were added over front doors, adding a graceful new touch to the elaborated Georgian entryway. Round-arched windows and passageways were introduced on the interiors, as were decorative "garlands" and delicate carved detailing.

Today, after several centuries of active use and modification, truly "pure" examples of any of the three principal styles of colonial New England—Medieval English, Georgian, or Federal—are quite rare. The few original or authentically restored Medieval examples are today mostly cherished museums—Salem's House of Seven Gables and Boston's Paul Revere House are two favorites. Many more relatively unmodified Georgian houses survive, but even these have usually received at least a Federal doorway or interior "redecoration" of some important room. Most have also been expanded by later additions or wings. Authentic Federal examples are more common, although many of these have also had later alteration.

Because of their age, and the usual paucity of early architectural records, it can be quite complex to figure out the precise history of any particular early New England house. Even a trained architectural historian might spend several weeks working on its genealogy and precise physical changes. Fortunately, the Society for the Preservation of New England Antiquities operates the Conservation Center, whose purpose is to help owners determine their house's history—what parts are original, or are architecturally significant additions, and how the building can be adapted for modern use without violating its historic integrity. The Center is located at 185 Lyman Street in Waltham, Massachusetts.

Many of the sixteen houses described on the following pages probably started out as simple, unadorned *folk houses* that lacked fashionable stylistic decoration. Both Chestnut Brook Farm and the Mary Ballantyne Ashley House may have been first built with the early Medieval room plan of two-over-two rooms, and later received a typical two-room saltbox addition on the rear. A third saltbox example, the Thomas Perkins House, was probably first built with this distinctive roof form.

Six of the houses in the book appear to have been first built with the larger four-over-four massed room plan, a shape that has come to be called the New England Large. These examples are the Thomas Buckingham House, the Captain Amos Palmer House, the Joseph Reynolds House, the Matthew Harvey House, the Elijah Wright House, and the Farnsworth house. An excellent demonstration of the range of decorative detailing found on New England Large houses can be seen by comparing the Wright and Palmer houses. The Elijah Wright House, although built rather late (1792) and at a time when the fashionable Federal style was dominant in urban areas, is essentially an unadorned folk house with little exterior detailing. The Captain Amos Palmer House of 1787, by contrast, has an elaborate Georgian facade. It is raised from the ground with an elegant front stoop and stairs, and has handsome decorative doorways both front and rear. Following damage from the War of 1812, it also received fine Federal interior detailing.

A still more elegantly elaborated example is the Vernon House, a 1758 Georgian with rich stylistic details both inside and out. This house also adds a center hallway to the four-rooms-per-floor pattern of the New England Large.

A somewhat less typical house shape is illustrated by the Isaac Peck House and the John Banks House. These are two-story dwellings with off-centered doorways and only three, rather than the usual four, ranks of windows. This form is known as the three-quarters house.

One house has a Federal style exterior. The lovely 1811 Parsonage was first built in the Federal style, easily identified by the characteristic fanlight above the front door. The Joseph Reynolds House, originally built in 1695, received a Federal remodeling of the front door in the early 1800s.

Three final examples illustrate still later modifications of early New England buildings. The Sabbath Day House was once a small meeting house, now moved and altered to become a cozy dwelling. The Reconstructed Colonial is a restoration of an early house and a store that were moved and joined to make a single large house. A third example, Charlescote Farm, incorporates an early Georgian core into a dramatically expanded Colonial Revival house built in 1903.

Browsing the pages of *The New England Colonial* calls up many evocative images of our nation's past. Reading the informative text reinforces those images by bringing to life the early settlers of New England and the rigors of conquering a new land. The sturdy houses they constructed have been occupied for over two centuries and still today provide unique charm, comfort, and even luxury to their fortunate occupants.

VIRGINIA AND LEE McALESTER,
Authors of
A Field Guide to American Houses

MASSACHUSETTS

When the Pilgrims sailed into what is now Plymouth, Massachusetts, in the winter of 1620, they faced a hostile, rugged wilderness and bitterly cold climate. As the _Mayflower_ nosed its way along the coastline, the 102 men, women, and children must have been struck by the thought that the only comforts of civilization they could now count on were limited to what they had brought with them.

Although nearly half the Pilgrims died during the first months, their settlement took hold. More successful were the well-financed efforts of the Massachusetts Bay Company, which between 1629 and 1630 brought over 1,200 English Puritans to settle villages, which later became Salem, Boston, Charlestown, and Medford. By 1643 some 20,000 settlers would arrive in the Massachusetts Bay Colony, which took its name from the Massachusets Indians, who lived around Boston Bay. Many of the settlers were financially comfortable Puritans who'd left England because of their differences with the Anglican church. Others wanted a better life than they'd known in turbulent seventeenth-century England, where government corruption prevailed, unemployment was staggering, and, for the half of the population living at poverty level, owning a home and land were beyond reach. The prospect of land to farm and timber to build a house was a great lure that sent men journeying across the ocean to the new settlements of the Massachusetts Bay Colony.

Besides the material possessions the Pilgrims and Puritans managed to bring across the ocean, they brought memory of the traditions of the southeastern English counties many originally came from. Memory was a powerful force, and the settlers' first instinct was to build on the forested New England coast the same styles of houses they had known in Essex, Suffolk, and Hertfordshire. Straight off the ships, they built temporary thatched hovels that probably resembled the basic dwellings of agricultural workers in seventeenth-century England. These were followed by permanent wood-frame houses. The settlers' building traditions were Elizabethan, based on the medieval technique of mortise and tenon joinery. The Eliz-

abethan half-timber house, with its oak support structure showing through white limestone walls, topped by a thatched roof, was perfectly suited to the more temperate English climate. The biting cold New England winter was another matter.

Anyone visiting the replicas of the thatched-roof structures, which stand today at Plimoth Plantation restoration in Plymouth, Massachusetts, will see how unsuitable the houses would have been in surviving a New England winter. Fierce winds would have lashed through the wattle and daub used to insulate the walls; the thatched roof would not have long withstood snow or the gale force winds whipping in from the northeast. Forced by necessity to adapt the English structure, the colonists protected the exterior sides of the house with horizontal clapboards and replaced the thatch with sturdier wood shingles. Windows were made small to keep out as much draft as possible. Glass was expensive, and those who couldn't afford glass and lead-paned windows relied on oiled paper or shutters as window covering.

The earliest Massachusetts colonial houses generally consisted of one or two ground floor rooms built around a central fireplace, which was kept burning continuously to provide heat, light, and cooking power. Upstairs, there were two loft-space rooms. The house's massive oak frame was clearly visible inside, with the hand-hewn posts and beams showing in a straightforward way exactly how the structure was held up. The two ground floor rooms were called the parlor, or best room, and the hall, or keeping room. Eventually, a lean-to might be attached at the back of the house. It might contain a kitchen in the center, a dairy at one end, and a small bedroom at the other end. Covered by a dramatically slanted roof, the shape of the entire structure seemed to have the appearance of the box the settlers stored salt in. It wasn't long before this saltbox house evolved into a native New England architectural style that was repeated throughout the New England colonies.

But in Massachusetts, certain English traditions continued to hold fast. Seventeenth-century houses are still standing today in Essex, Salem, and Boston that have severely pointed gables and a second story that juts out sharply over the ground floor. Most famous of these houses is the Turner-Ingersoll House, which inspired Nathaniel Hawthorne's *House of Seven Gables*. The jutting second story was an English medieval construction style, well suited to crowded English town streets, where it allowed for a more roomy upper story. Between 1650 and 1700, the severe gabled house with a second story overhang became a style favored by Puritan families whose growing prosperity allowed them to build new houses or remodel their original two-room houses in this design.

As the settlements became established and prosperity increased, some seventeenth-century houses reflected well-to-do comfort. The inventory for the parlor of one Roxbury house recorded thirteen chairs with leather seats, six chairs with colorful carpeted seats known as Turkey work, and four stools with needlework covers. In rural houses, furnishings would have been more modest, and it would not even have been unusual to see the family chickens being fed in the keeping room.

In both modest and prosperous houses, the hall, or keeping room, was the scene of most day-to-day living. Furnishings would include chairs, tables, and cupboards, as well as tools and some farm equipment. Although no particular room was designated for dining—the term "dining room" was not common until after the Revolution—most meals would be taken in the keeping room, which also contained the implements for cooking and eating. The parlor, which showed off the family's best furniture, was the room the family entertained in. It would also boast the best bed in the house, since this was where the parents slept. The rest of the family would have slept in the upstairs loft spaces, although it would not have been uncommon to see a bed in the keeping room, as well.

The approach of the 1700s brought significant changes in Massachusetts. In 1691 the English reorganized Massachusetts Bay as a royal colony and installed a royal governor in Boston. By then a thriving port, Boston had become the main nerve center of trade for the New England colonies. The new, more prosperous and expansive attitude of the Massachusetts Colony was beginning to be reflected in its domestic architecture. Old medieval building techniques were waning, giving way to the classic and gracious Georgian house.

The new house was a four-room plan two-story structure. Its pleasingly symmetrical layout was dominated by a spacious central hallway, with harmoniously balanced chimneys rising at each end of the house. The roofline had a graceful slope. Instead of the narrow casement windows of the seventeenth-century house, there were now larger sash windows. Inside the house, ceilings were raised and rooms became more spacious. Walls were plastered and beams that were once exposed were concealed with casing boards. Fine detailing appeared in the form of moldings and raised-panel woodwork. The yawning hearth that was a feature of seventeenth-century houses was downsized in a practical move to throw more heat into the room. The change resulted in a more elegant fireplace, too. Rough-hewn shelves that had been used to store china in the seventeenth-century house were replaced with built-in corner cupboards sporting carved molding and pilasters. Interior

woodwork was often enlivened with painted imitations of wood graining and marble.

In the eighteenth-century house, rooms became more specialized in function. Two of the ground floor rooms served as parlors—the "best" parlor and the more frequently used "common" parlor—while the others served as a kitchen and a keeping room. The upstairs rooms were now entirely given over to sleeping, with the parents occupying the main bedroom. In prosperous houses, the main bedroom was comfortably, even elegantly, furnished. It might have a highboy, which stored clothing and linens, and a lowboy, which served as a dressing table. There might be an upholstered chair. Now known as the wing chair, the eighteenth-century chair was intended for the elderly or infirm, and always kept in the bedroom.

Furniture also became more specialized in its functions, reflecting increased wealth and leisure. The seventeenth-century trestle table had been designed so that it could be disassembled and stored when not in use. But in the eighteenth century, furniture was often left set up, intended to be admired. The best example of this is the tea table, which usually stood in the best parlor, permanently set with a complete tea service.

The fine mahogany and walnut furniture that now appeared in prosperous Massachusetts houses was often fashioned in Boston rather than imported from London. Immigrants trained in the cabinetry arts of London had arrived in Boston, transforming the city into a furniture-making center of renown that supplied the other colonies and competed successfully with London. By the 1740s Boston cabinetmakers, as well as those in Newport, Rhode Island, had developed and perfected the blocked-front dressing tables and desks that represent the highest artistic achievement of New England colonial cabinetmaking.

The latest fashions in furniture and decorating arrived in Boston, and were eventually carried into the more rural parts of Massachusetts, where they were imitated by country artisans. The shift to Georgian styles did not occur overnight, however. Nor did the frugal New Englanders suddenly toss aside their seventeenth-century possessions. The transition was gradual and uneven. Often new Georgian panelling and woodwork was superimposed on sturdy old seventeenth-century structures. A furniture style might be perpetuated in the country long after it had ceased to be popular in Boston or Salem. Often the country artisan abbreviated the design or added idiosyncratic flourishes of his own. Social and economic differences between the city and country were great. Fishing, trading, and shipbuilding brought prosperity to port cities and seacoast towns, creating thriving economies that sup-

ported artisans and tradesmen. But many Massachusetts colonists lived inland on farms, where life might be more simple.

Yet the influence of changing architectural and interior styles did reach far into the rural Massachusetts landscape. All of the colonial Massachusetts homes on the following pages are country houses. Most rural of all is the Mary Ballantyne Ashley House, built in the far western Massachusetts Berkshires in 1740. Although it started out as a basic saltbox, one room was later updated with Georgian raised panelling. The change reflects the owner's growing prosperity as much as the advance of fashion. The two farmhouses in Sherborn show how styles evolved within the same town. The clapboard farmhouse at Chestnut Brook Farm is a late-seventeenth-century two-over-two plan with a later saltbox lean-to addition. Its straightforward style contrasts significantly with Charlescote Farm, which combines an original Georgian core with Colonial Revival and contemporary additions.

The houses of colonial Massachusetts that survive today are an irreplaceable heritage. Their forms and details are worth contemplating for their aesthetic appeal. But that beauty is all the more compelling when we realize that these houses are living history that mirror the tastes, styles, and customs of the colonial times that created them.

Chestnut Brook Farm

A SIMPLE 1703 SALTBOX IN SHERBORN

Located approximately twenty miles southwest of Boston, between the Charles River and Dopping Brook, Sherborn was established in the 1650s as a small English settlement of some twenty inhabitants. Originally known as Boggestow, or Boggestown, a name that makes reference to the boggy lowlands the early settlers found ideal for cranberry cultivation, the town was incorporated as "Sherborne" in 1674 and has retained that name—though with a variation in spelling—to the present.

The early development of Sherborn, and indeed of the entire Massachusetts Bay Colony, was temporarily halted in 1675 by King Philip's War, a devastating Indian uprising that was waged to push the settlers back to the beachheads and regain land long held by Indian tribes. Before the war ended in 1676, fighting spread to Connecticut and Rhode Island. Led by Philip, sachem of the Wampanoags, and eventually fought by the Nipmucks and Narragansets as well, this conflict destroyed thirteen Massachusetts settlements and damaged a half dozen more.

Philip was the younger son of Massasoit (1580–1660), the Wampanoag chief who in 1621 signed the earliest recorded treaty with the Pilgrims and who remained the staunchest of their Indian allies until his death nearly forty years later. Perhaps because of his allegiance with the settlers, Massasoit gave English names to his two sons, Alexander and Philip, both of whom succeeded him as leader of the Wam-

Standing in winter splendor like a Currier & Ives print of an early New England homestead, Chestnut Brook Farm dates from 1703 (LEFT). The original structure was a simple two rooms over two rooms wrapped around a central chimney. A saltbox lean-to and a stone structure at the back of the house were added later in the eighteenth century.

The striking front door (RIGHT), set off with wide carved molding, is considerably more elaborate than the simple clapboard farmhouse, and was probably added around 1820.

panoags. Philip, the younger son, became sachem in 1662. He renewed the treaties his father had made with the Pilgrims and honored those treaties for nearly ten years. But threatened by the encroachment of the colonists' growing settlements, Philip had organized by 1675 a confederation of Indian tribes into a formidable fighting force. The Indians attacked the western Massachusetts settlements around Brookfield and within months pushed the theater of war east to the outskirts of Boston and Providence. The tide turned in the colonists' favor with the destruction of the Narragansets' fort and eventual execution of the Narraganset sachem, Canon Chet. The war ended four months later when King Philip was killed during a surprise attack by colonists. The war devastated the Massachusetts Bay Colony settlements. One thousand colonists died and the western frontier of 1675 would not be reached again for another twenty years.

Throughout the autumn and winter of 1676, colonists in Sherborn, as in other Massachusetts Bay settlements, rebuilt their farms and returned to the business of establishing their communities. In 1679 Sherborn's first sawmill was constructed. The first schoolhouse was built in 1728, and by 1750, 643 settlers were living in Sherborn.

Chestnut Brook Farm is one of the houses that Sherborn claims from this period of growth just after King Philip's War. The builder of the house and its original ownership cannot be documented through town records. But it is known that twenty-four acres of the land beside Chestnut Brook were assigned to Thomas Sawin, the builder of Sherborn's first sawmill. It is unclear whether it was Sawin who built the house or members of the Bullen family, who occupied the prop-

The owners commissioned this watercolor of Chestnut Brook Farm (ABOVE) from Anne Bell Robb, a Sherborn artist who specializes in colonial themes.

At the foot of the drive a sign announces the way to Chestnut Brook Farm. Now a guest house, this structure is the oldest building on the property, dating from the seventeenth century when it served as a forge and cobbler's shop (RIGHT).

14

In the guest cottage, the robust colonial fireplace and exposed posts and beams are hallmarks of the seventeenth-century colonial building technique. In front of the fire is a comfortable nineteenth-century painted rocking chair.

The built-in beds were added in the 1930s when the building became a guest cottage. With its sparse rustic furniture, the room conveys an idea of what the slope-roofed sleeping quarters of the Massachusetts Bay Colony's earliest houses might have looked like in the seventeenth century.

erty in the early 1700s. The precise date of construction is also unclear; the period between 1680 and 1712 is most often suggested. Historical records do show that a child was born on the property in 1700 and that by the early 1800s a house on the property had been sold to Galem Bullard, a successful stone mason.

Today Chestnut Brook Farm is the home of Steve Petty, a builder, and Kitty Petty, a school teacher, and their children, Sarah and Andrew. The Pettys purchased the house in 1978 to operate as a small working farm, where they raise Hereford beef cattle and grow Christmas trees.

It was the Pettys who christened the property Chestnut Brook Farm. Chestnut Brook was the original name of Course Brook, the stream that winds through the property. Because of the farm's association with Sherborn's earliest days, the Pettys reached back into history for an appropriate house name.

Like most colonial New England farmhouses, this one has been added to over the years, and the exact dates of those additions have been lost in time. The original structure, built around a central chimney, was erected as two rooms over two—the spaces that are now the living room and dining room, and two rooms upstairs. The house was then expanded with an undated saltbox addition across the rear. The Pettys believe the next portion of the house to be added was a stone section at the rear, which is attached today, but was at first a separate outbuilding. The house remained much in its original state until 1930 when it was renovated and modernized with heat, electricity, water, and a new kitchen and bathrooms.

Seeming to graze in the snow, the wrought iron sculpture of a ram outside the back door of Chestnut Brook Farm was a wedding present. The rustic stone structure in the background was once a separate outbuilding, but at some point well over 125 years ago it was attached to the house. It now is a bedroom (FAR LEFT).

This little red outbuilding (ABOVE LEFT) is used as a workshop and a shelter for newly born animals.

A bird feeder provides a wintry perch for a ruddy brown female cardinal (ABOVE RIGHT).

The slant front desk and Windsor chairs in the living room (FAR LEFT) once stood in the Illinois house of Kitty Petty's grandfather. Like the Chinese export porcelains in the nearby cabinet, they date from the late-eighteenth and early-nineteenth century. The inviting fireplace, framed in the original eighteenth-century raised panelling, is one of four in the house.

Although it has the aged look of an antique, the table in the dining room is a new one, crafted in the American Shaker style, which the owners commissioned for the room. The Windsor chairs are modern reproductions. The mellow pine panelling on the wall dates from the eighteenth century (LEFT).

The oldest building on the property is not the farmhouse, however, but a separate small structure, now used as a guest house, which stands close to the road. In the seventeenth century, this building housed a forge on the lower level and a cobbler's shop above. The structure became a guest cottage in the improvements in the 1930s.

The Pettys have made their own improvements, often removing alterations made by previous owners in the early-twentieth century who unwittingly covered up original colonial architectural features. Steve Petty had always guessed that the lean-to kitchen must have had a fireplace, even though the room appeared to have none when the couple purchased the house. His hunch proved correct when he investigated a crawlspace and discovered that a past owner had walled up the handsome colonial kitchen hearth. Kitty Petty made her own discovery when she pulled away two layers of lath and plaster from the woodwork around the first floor stairway, revealing a sheathed wall that probably dates from the house's original construction. The couple's investigations have also revealed that most of the house is built of chestnut wood.

Today, the interiors have an inviting warmth. The Pettys have captured the spirit of an early New England farmhouse by filling the rooms with arrangements of antiques and country-style colonial reproductions. With the early rustic woodwork and detailing now revealed, the rooms are appealing colonial backdrops for the Petty's busy lives. The lean-to hearth is now the place where the family gathers after cross-country skiing. The early stone section at the rear of the house, perhaps once an ice house or storage room for the kitchen, is now the bedroom of the Petty's son Andrew. The barn was reconstructed on the foundation of the old chestnut barn with pine and oak from the property and is today part of the Petty's cattle operation. Humming with family activity and farm life, the old buildings of Chestnut Brook Farm keep their age and history tangibly alive in the present.

21

Kitty Petty dug down through two layers of plaster and lath to find the sheathing of the stairway (NEAR RIGHT). This simple, slightly rustic sheathing is typical of the interior construction in the oldest colonial New England houses. The original wideboard floors are pine.

On cold days, the Pettys come in from the back entrance to warm themselves by the fire in the room that was the lean-to kitchen in the eighteenth century (FAR TOP RIGHT). The owners uncovered the fireplace and panelled fireplace wall, which were concealed under lath that was probably added early in the twentieth century.

A snowy farmyard scene is populated by one of the Petty's fourteen Hereford beef cattle. The farm equipment in the background is a vintage manure spreader of unknown date that came to the Petty's from a neighboring farmer (FAR BOTTOM RIGHT).

22

Mary Ballantyne Ashley House

A 1738 SALTBOX IN THE BERKSHIRE MOUNTAINS

The Konkapit River, a well-travelled waterway in colonial times, originally ran behind the house, which was first occupied by a miller. The river's course was diverted in the 1840s when the first railway tracks were laid in the Berkshires. The sloped roof of the 1738 saltbox is just visible through the trees (LEFT).

The structural framework of the Mary Ballantyne Ashley House is chestnut, a hardwood that, along with oak, was a favored building material in colonial New England. The simple elegance of the doorway trim is typical of the early colonial Georgian style (RIGHT).

Nestled in the shadows of the Berkshire Mountains, the Mary Ballantyne Ashley House was built in 1738 as a miller's house by Captain John Ashley. Captain Ashley (1669–1759) was a noted figure in the Massachusetts Colony; a man who, like the son and grandson who would also bear his name, played a role in shaping the colony's history. Captain Ashley was a member of the court-appointed committee that purchased the land that would eventually encompass the towns of Sheffield, Great Barrington, Egremont, West Stockbridge, and Lee. The land was purchased from Chief Konkapot, leader of the Mahican Indian tribe, in 1724 for 460 pounds, three barrels of cider, and thirty quarts of rum.

Captain John Ashley's son, Colonel John Ashley (1709–1802), was for twenty years judge of the Court of Common Pleas of Berkshire County and established the first county courthouse in Great Barrington. He is perhaps best known for the battle he waged to declare slavery illegal in Massachusetts under the new Massachusetts constitution of 1780. Captain Ashley's grandson, Major General John Ashley (1736–1799), also played a role in Berkshires history: in 1786 he led the federal militia in suppressing rebelling farmers in the uprising that came to be known as Shay's Rebellion.

Savvy entrepreneurs, the Ashleys launched some of the first industry in the Berkshires. The captain created a local iron mill that made armaments during the Revolution. There were also wheat mills,

Now a back patio just off the first floor master bedroom, the rear section of the house was an open-to-the-outdoors wheelwright shop in the 1800s. The massive hand-hewn beam runs the entire length of the wing (LEFT).

The eighteenth-century dairy, or buttery, was converted into a kitchen (ABOVE). Because modern kitchen cabinets would be jarring in a historic house, a local cabinet-maker created eighteenth-century style raised panel cabinets. The cabinets form a suitable backdrop for the owners' antique kitchen utensils and collection of old baskets, which hang from an original overhead beam.

grist mills, and other small Ashley factories dotting the Konkapot River, which fed into the Housatonic. Since river transportation was frequently more reliable in colonial times than overland routes, early industry burgeoned along New England's rivers. Thus in 1738, Captain Ashley chose a site on the banks of the Konkapit River to build a house for the miller who operated one of the Ashleys' grist mills. The center chimney house with a saltbox lean-to was strategically located at an overland crossroads, too. To the east lay the way to Boston, to the south were the western Connecticut Berkshire settlements, to the north, those of the Massachusetts Berkshires. Well into the nineteenth century the house was a nucleus of commerce. In the 1800s a blacksmith's shop and wheelwright's shop were established. Attached to the house, the wheelwright shop was open to the air so that wagons could be driven in to be repaired, making the house a sort of colonial-style gas station.

Until the 1750s the house was occupied by employees of the Ashley family, first the miller and then various workers who were involved with the iron works. At some point in the 1750s Major General John Ashley moved into the house with his second wife, Mary Ballantyne Ashley. For the next hundred years the house remained in Ashley hands, passing to one or another of the Major General's eight children. In 1858 the house was sold to a J. S. Pease, and later in the nineteenth century it belonged to a family named Moons, who retained it until the turn of the century. There were several owners from the 1900s to the 1960s, when the house became the weekend residence of a New York antiques dealer who preserved it with much

Structurally unaltered since the eighteenth century, the original low-ceilinged keeping room with its huge hearth now serves as an inviting living room (FAR LEFT). The mantel is decorated with a collection of eighteenth- and nineteenth-century pewter. Modern reproduction wing chairs provide comfortable fireside seating.

A nineteenth-century mahogany rolltop desk is tucked into the second story landing to create an office (LEFT). The original saltbox had two large upstairs rooms that were partitioned as the house was updated and a bathroom was added.

29

An opening in the guest bathroom (RIGHT) leads to a secret chamber built next to the central chimney. Called "the Indian hole," it was probably a hiding place built in case of Indian attack. The original entrance may have been hidden behind panelling.

In the 1960s a previous owner converted the space that had been the wheelwright's shop into a well-insulated master bedroom (FAR RIGHT). The tiger maple four-poster bed and grain-painted blanket chest at the foot of the bed are nineteenth-century American pieces; the portrait of the child is an English naive painting dating from the eighteenth century.

needed structural restoration work. In the 1970s the house was sold to the present owners, Dorothy and Howard Crockett.

For 250 years the house has retained much of its original saltbox shape and layout. Built around the central chimney on the first floor are the original kitchen, or keeping room, now used as a living room, and the best parlor, now the dining room. Two decades ago the nineteenth-century wheelwright's shop was enclosed, well-insulated, and transformed into the first floor master bedroom. The colonial buttery, originally in the saltbox lean-to, was converted by the present owners into the kitchen. The second floor, which would have been two open loft spaces in the eighteenth century, now has two bedrooms, an office at the top of the stairs, and a small room with a steeply slanted ceiling that may have once been upstairs sleeping quarters. Upstairs and downstairs bathrooms have also been added.

One of the most interesting qualities about the house is the way the interior construction reveals the evolution of colonial building styles. The old keeping room still has the exposed beams and yawning hearth that are earmarks of the medieval-rooted seventeenth-century style of colonial construction. The dining room, however, features the raised panelling and smaller hearth that became stylish in the early-eighteenth century. No doubt altered after the Ashleys moved into the miller's house in the 1750s, the dining room shows how, even in this woodsy Berkshire outpost, homeowners strove to keep up with interior design fashions. The addition of the panelling is a sign of the Ashley family's prosperity and stature in the community.

Another intriguing detail about the house is its secret room

Howard Crockett's fondness for timepieces and maritime objects is apparent in the clocks and paintings grouped around the staircase (TOP RIGHT). The clock on the far left was made by Silas Hoadley in Connecticut around 1812, while that on the right was probably made by Aaron Willard, or one of his sons, in the mid-1800s. Next to it is a nineteenth-century papier-mâché mannequin's head.

The bay window in the dining room (BOTTOM RIGHT) is a twentieth-century alteration added some thirty years ago by previous owners. The sculptural wood carving of a pineapple on the window sill is an English trade sign. The pineapple was an eighteenth-century symbol of hospitality and welcome.

The addition of the French Empire sofa to the living room (TOP RIGHT) is an eclectic European touch that is quite compatible with the room's American furniture—the nineteenth-century drop leaf table near the window and, in the corner, the desk dating from about 1860. A model of a colonial slave ship, a Baltimore clipper called Dos Amigos, sits in a glass case.

In the dining room, an anonymous portrait of an unknown sea captain dating from about 1790 hangs on the panelled fireplace wall (BOTTOM RIGHT). The owner has decorated the mantel with maritime objects a sea captain of that era might have owned, including a chronometer, a sextant, an ebony and ivory checkerboard, and a shipmaster's "rattle." Fitted into the fireplace is an early-nineteenth-century sea captain's stove, trimmed in brass and ornamented with Dutch tile work.

The charming garden designed by Dorothy Crockett is a spot of tranquility among the towering and ancient New England trees (TOP).

This sculptural metal design (ABOVE) is reminiscent of a waterwheel and is displayed in the garden as a tip of the hat to the Ashley grist mill that figured so prominently in Berkshire colonial commerce and the history of the house.

The owner has turned the first floor of the barn into his private den (RIGHT), where he often retreats to enjoy his collection of maritime objects and read the volumes that are part of his library on physics, astronomy, and navigational aids. The library table is a draper's table that once stood in a nineteenth-century Connecticut department store. He discovered it by chance in an old warehouse where it had been stored and forgotten.

Once a vital part of a bustling blacksmith and wagon repair business in the nineteenth century, the barn now serves as a library retreat (FAR RIGHT). When guests come to stay, they are often put up in the barn's second story.

which can accommodate four to six people. It is built in the huge vaulted chimney. House tradition has referred to the space as "the Indian hole," and several owners have guessed that it was intended as a hiding place in case of Indian attack. Since the area was well populated with Indians throughout the mid-eighteenth century, that is a likely possibility. Another concealed space is found behind the panelled dining room wall and is accessible through a removable stair in the attic staircase. The space may have been a hiding place for both people and valuables. Or, as the present owners surmise, it may have been used for eavesdropping on conversations in the dining room. As the best parlor, the dining room would probably have been used for meetings about local business and political affairs. Considering the Ashley family's role in Berkshire politics, particularly during the Revolution, the possibility of a concealed chamber for eavesdropping may not be farfetched.

Today, the Crocketts are dedicated and enthusiastic caretakers of the Mary Ballantyne Ashley house's traditions. They have filled the rooms with furniture and accessories that span the eighteenth and nineteenth centuries, creating a warm period atmosphere appropriate to the house's age. The barn that was once part of a thriving wagon-repair business has been turned into an office and guest cottage. And the well-tended grounds now boast an herb garden inspired by the owners' many trips to England. Today the house is well loved and lived in as it must have been in the eighteenth century when the Ashley family was in residence.

35

Charlescote Farm

A 1759 GEORGIAN ESTATE OUTSIDE OF BOSTON

T he quintessential gentleman's country estate, Charlescote Farm is one of those idyllic properties that were developed in Sherborn in the early 1900s as the summer retreats of wealthy Bostonians. Encompassing more than 300 acres adjoining the Charles River and graced by a house that is both elegant and grand without the slightest hint of pretention, Charlescote Farm is the sort of place anyone with a love of New England's countryside would like to call home.

Not only is it a beautiful house, it is also an historic one: the oldest portion of the house was built in 1759 by Joshua Morse, a descendant of one of Sherborn's first settlers. The farm may be the site of one of Sherborn's earliest homesteads. Joshua was descended from Daniel Morse, Sr., a farmer whose home, built on or very near the site Joshua Morse chose, served as a garrison house during King Philip's War. Well respected among his fellow pioneers, Daniel Morse was elected one of the settlement's first selectmen. Both Farm Road and Farm Pond, designations of longstanding on Sherborn maps, draw their names from the property that Daniel Morse called simply The Farm.

The original house Joshua Morse built on the site was Georgian in style, its large square rooms constructed in a center-hall, two-story plan. The 1700s brought the Georgian influence to colonial New England architecture. Distinguished by graceful lines and proportions,

Resplendent in the snowy New England countryside, the core of Charlescote Farm dates from 1759 when Joshua Morse established his family farm in Sherborn. Colonial Revival additions were grafted onto the original section of the house (LEFT) in the early 1900s.

A winter snow turns the gardens of Charlescote Farm into a white fairyland (RIGHT).

houses of this period featured carved molding, raised panelling, and elegantly carved mantelpieces. Although later alterations were made to the interiors and exteriors of the Morse house, the original Georgian core has been elegantly complemented by the large Colonial Revival addition of the early 1900s and the contemporary addition of recent years.

The house remained in the Morse family until 1903 when it was sold to a Dr. Channing who engaged the Boston architect Joseph Everett Chandler to enlarge it. Regarded as an authority on colonial architecture, Joseph Everett Chandler worked on many historic landmarks in Massachusetts throughout his career. His work on the Joshua Morse house included designing a large Colonial Revival addition at the north side and creating a porte cochère along the south end. The Colonial Revival that swept America in the early-twentieth century brought an appreciation for colonial architecture and decorative arts, which had fallen out of favor during most of the nineteenth century.

The back of the house shows twentieth-century alterations (LEFT). The bow-shaped window is probably part of the Colonial Revival renovation undertaken in the early 1900s by the Boston architect Joseph Everett Chandler. The rounded extension on the far right is the most recent alteration, designed in 1981 by the architect James Walker.

Displayed in the dining room's bay window (ABOVE) is Sally Willis's mother's collection of ruby glass, including several goblets, a decanter, and a pair of horn-shaped vases, all made between 1840 and 1900.

The revival led to the rescue of many colonial buildings and pieces of furniture, as well as to the adaptation of these designs in new houses and furnishings.

Joseph Everett Chandler's expansion of the Joshua Morse house is believed to have set the precedent for the conversion of other houses in the area to grand country estates. It was around this time that Sherborn's southern and eastern areas witnessed the development of estate properties used primarily as summer homes, when many houses built during earlier phases of Sherborn's history were transformed into larger, more gracious summer retreats. This period saw much of the building activity that Sherborn would experience during the twentieth century. Because many of Sherborn's early roads were not upgraded until after World War II, and because sizable portions of land were devoted to agriculture or retained by estate owners, the town has preserved a tranquil, rural character longer than many other towns nearby.

A few years following the completion of the architect's expansion, the property was acquired by the Saltonstalls, who used the house as their weekend and summer residence. Richard Saltonstall named the property Charlescote Farm, a term of his own invention that, in French, combines the name Charles, from the Charles River, with the word côté—thus, "by the side of the Charles." The farm was subsequently owned by the Saltonstalls' son and daughter-in-law, who lived there during the 1920s. In 1982, the farm became the property of their daughter, Sally Willis, and she, her husband, Dudley, and their four children have lived at Charlescote Farm ever since.

The Willises have continued Charlescote Farm's tradition of being a working farm by raising Hereford beef cattle and producing a substantial crop of hay. They have also continued the process of modifying the house to suit their needs, just as Dr. Channing did at the turn of the century and the Saltonstalls did in the 1920s. With four active children, the Willises found that they needed a playroom. They also discovered that the old kitchen did not suit their life-style. With a warren of pantries isolated from the rest of the house, it had been designed for an era when a staff ran the kitchen and the lady of the house entered it mostly to give instructions to the cook. The Willises' recent renovation, designed by architect James Walker of Dover, Massachusetts, opened up the kitchen area and linked it more directly with the other parts of the house and provided for a second story children's playroom. The showpiece of the architect's design is the soaring two-story circular tower that was added to the kitchen to create a breakfast area downstairs and a balcony extension for the

As it has been for over 200 years, Charlescote Farm is maintained today as a working farm. Here, some of the owners' seventy-five Hereford beef cattle are seen in front of the largest of the farm's barns (LEFT). Several other outbuildings and small houses are clustered on the property.

A walnut flintlock American musket and brass powder flask, both from the nineteenth century, hang over the fireplace in what is now the entrance hall (RIGHT). The oil painting on the wall by the nineteenth-century artist Joseph Foxcroft Cole is entitled Landscape with Cows—*a fitting image for Charlescote Farm. The antique copper warming pan and tea kettle add a lustrous glow.*

The sitting room (RIGHT) is comfortably furnished with a mixture of reproduction and antique family pieces. The Chippendale style settee, with carved knees and pad feet, is an early-twentieth-century reproduction. The bench is upholstered in a needlework design stitched by Sally Willis's mother, showing the Saltonstall family, including Sally as a baby, assembled at Charlescote Farm.

A vignette of family curios arranged on the upper shelves of an Empire desk includes a collection of small boxes, silhouettes and miniature portraits, small porcelains, and a decorated leather bound book (FAR RIGHT).

second floor playroom. The slightly exaggerated appearance of the two-story mullioned windows imparts a rather Post Modern contemporary look to the addition, yet their curved Palladian shape harmonizes with the rest of the house.

The main living areas of Charlescote Farm radiate from the center hall and front foyer, which is the oldest section of the house, dating from 1759. Sofas have been re-covered and rooms have been repainted, but otherwise the Willises have kept the main living areas as they were when Sally Willis was growing up. Rooms are filled with family possessions. Some are antique. But many, such as Sally Willis's mother's needlework and the head of the moose shot by Dudley Willis's grandfather, are family mementos. These personal objects give the rooms of Charlescote Farm a welcoming, informal warmth. As Sally Willis says, Charlescote Farm is "a big, happy, family house," and by including such family mementos she has injected vibrancy into the house's colonial rooms. Voicing a thought that must have occurred to Joshua Morse when he first built the farm in 1759, Sally Willis imagines a time when her own children might want to bring their families to live at Charlescote Farm. "When you think about it, that's what these houses have been about for all these years."

Looking down from the second story playroom balcony to the kitchen breakfast area gives a dramatic view of the 1981 kitchen alteration designed by architect James Walker (LEFT). The built-in banquette is upholstered in French provincial cotton. The moosehead surveying the scene is "Ike," a trophy that, according to family tradition, was bagged by Dudley Willis's grandfather, Isaac, in 1920 in Colorado.

In the guest room, colonial style sconces cast a candlelike glow on the Sheraton dressing table, creating a sense of what nighttime indoor lighting might have been like in the eighteenth century (TOP).

Added in 1920, the den (ABOVE) was designed with panelled woodwork and a colonial style fireplace that blends with the original eighteenth-century section of the house. The sets of books on literature and history have been in the owners' families for decades.

Warmed by a crackling fire, the dining room (RIGHT) is set up for a formal dinner, with stencilled American nineteenth-century Hitchcock chairs pulled around an English mahogany table that dates from about 1830.

CONNECTICUT

The first recorded European to discover Connecticut was Dutch navigator Adriaen Block. In 1614, representing the Dutch West India Company, he explored the lower Connecticut River, which was called Quonecktacut, meaning "long river of the pines," by the local Indians. A derivation of this name was soon attached to the surrounding territory. The Dutch, operating from New Amsterdam (later called New York), established a trading post in the center of present day Connecticut near Hartford in 1633.

Almost immediately, in the struggle for control of the American colonies as well as to establish bases for nonconforming religious beliefs, the English moved in. The first was the Leicestershire-born Reverend Thomas Hooker (1586–1647), who in 1634 brought his congregation from Massachusetts to Wetherfield, just south of Hartford. Hooker not only helped frame the state's constitution, "The Fundamental Orders of Connecticut," in 1638, but also established Congregationalism as the dominating religious sect for the state. A second Englishman, John Winthrop (1606–1676), established a colony at Saybrook at the mouth of the Connecticut River in 1635. He was to become governor of Connecticut and is known as the father of paper currency in America. In 1638 Coventry-born John Davenport (1597–1670) established New Haven. A tug of war between these settlements, battles with the area's Pequot Indians, and boundary disputes with Massachusetts, Rhode Island, and New York were not resolved until the last quarter of the eighteenth century when Connecticut finally formed its present geographic shape.

As with most New England towns, land settlement in Connecticut was formed by a system of metes and bounds. This is described by Allen G. Noble in *Wood, Brick, & Stone* as a plan that "produces irregular properties of uneven size." The subdivision of land was based on units of human measure, such as feet, paces and spans, and natural landmarks. Each New England town, a word which then referred to an area rather than an urban development, consisted of a village that, Noble says, "was the single major focus of the settlement and its surrounding agricultural fields. In the early agricultural market villages, the meetinghouse or hall and the adjacent local tavern provided the focal point for the settlements. Later on the now-familiar New England village form of public buildings and business establishments fronting on a central green or commons evolved."

The major difficulty for the earliest colonists was the clearing of land. They selected the land by the type of trees they found growing on it, according to John R. Stilgoe in *Common Landscape of America*. The inhabitants of the thirteen English colonies determined that only forested land had value, and of those forests, ". . . oak, hiskory (sic), walnut, cherry, black ash, elm, beech, and several other trees," listed one James Smith, a traveller to America in the 1750s, grew on the most sought after land. Most European visitors were shocked by what appeared to them to be the wanton destruction of virgin forests, for most of Europe had been cleared of forests long before their memory. Colonists used timbers for building and heating, and, from very early on, exported wood to England. Sawmills, powered by water or wind, were established and encouraged, though the early ones were run by farmers on a toll basis, more or less as a sideline, according to Oscar Theodore Barck, Jr., and Hugh Talmage Lefler in *Colonial America*. Millers were encouraged by special grants of lands, by exemption from local taxes, and sometimes by exemption from military duty.

In New England there was the added difficulty of clearing very rocky land. Usually the colonists piled rocks in rows equidistant from the center of their fields, Stilgoe writes, and though European visitors criticized the quality of the stone wall structures, the colonists were far more interested in land clearing than fence building. Because of this, their fields were quite small, for it took less time and labor to clear eight small fields and plant them than to clear one large field of the same acreage. Indeed, for many years crops had to be grown using methods closer to gardening than to our concept of farming. Axes, spades, and mattocks (a digging or grubbing instrument) were used rather than ploughs, which did not come into general use until the end of the seventeenth century. Even the grass native to the New World, though ferociously tall, was found to be unsuitable for winter fodder. Gradually English grasses, brought over in fodder and bedding, took hold and thrived in New England, where they are now thought of as indigenous.

Many houses in Connecticut, even in coastal areas, started out as farmhouses, though most of these were not intended to be permanent. Eventually, with prosperity, more enduring houses came about, often built by seafarers or merchants. Early in the eighteenth century, colonists' houses were made more colorful by being painted. Though considered at first to be a wealthy houseowner's indulgence, soon the less rich applied paint to prevent the wood of their houses from rotting or splitting. Newspapers in the more sophisticated coastal towns all over the eastern seaboard advertised "painter's colors," which were imported and included Indian red, olive green, pumpkin yellow, gray, and blue. Eventually, according to Stilgoe, very fancy shades such as Dutch pink and Naples yellow were available, but imports of these dropped sharply with the passing of the Stamp Act (1765), and the colonists in retaliation devised their own paint formulas. Of these, the most prevalent was Spanish brown, the dull red color that anticipated the rather more vivid red we now associate with red barns. At first, when paint was an expensive luxury, it was applied mainly to public buildings. Because the meetinghouse was the focal point, involving all the townsfolk in these one-religion settlements,

it was often the most colorful structure in the village. Stilgoe discovered that in 1762 the Connecticut town of Pomfret voted that "the meetinghouse should be colored on the outside of an orange color, the doors and bottom boards of a chocolate color, the windows, jets, corner boards and weather boards, colored white." Later, as individual citizens grew more affluent, their dwellings started to rival the public structures. By 1789, in the town of Woodbury, where the Sabbath House featured in this section is located, the citizens determined that its meetinghouse would be "near the color of Mr. Timothy Tomlinson's house except it be a little more greenish to it." It wasn't until the beginning of the nineteenth century that white, considered an expensive color to use, became popular. The wealthy painted their houses white all over, with green shutters. The less rich just painted the front of their houses. White buildings seemed to symbolize the New Republic, complete with its new Stars and Stripes and dollar currency. White suited the new classically-inspired architecture, and to this day, the color remains the most popular for New England's frame houses.

At first, the interiors of these houses were very simple and utilitarian. Furniture was made by hand from local woods and designed to be space-saving: a few stools, a long bench, a crude table, shelves, a larder for provisions, and a few pots and pans sufficed. Beds originally would have been little more than a mattress of leaves or straw; utensils were fashioned from iron, wood, or bone, dishes from wood, pewter, or crude earthenware. Many of these simple early furnishings have great appeal and a distinction that is typical of New England. Dower chests, hutch and sawbuck tables, corner cupboards, and wood cradles are much collected, as is the direct and evocative folk art that was produced in New England's country areas. The John Banks House in Fairfield, shown in this section, is full of such treasures.

Houses nearer to Connecticut's coastline built by those involved with the maritime trades tended to be larger and more sophisticated. The Thomas Buckingham House in Essex, and the Captain Amos Palmer House in Stonington are prime examples. Trade with Europe and the increasing China sea trade resulted in more cosmopolitan furnishings such as lacquered or japanned furniture and fine porcelain. Wills and inventories of the time indicate that some colonial houses were quite luxurious. Far from a mattress on the floor, bedsteads, often four-posters, might be fashioned from mahogany, walnut, pine, maple, or cherry. Indeed, apart from imported, finely carved English furniture, Connecticut produced some of its own distinctive furniture, made by skilled cabinetmakers, some of whom are featured in the Sabbath Day House, built in 1740 in Woodbury.

These four Connecticut houses give us in the 1980s a glimpse of colonial life in the eighteenth century.

John Banks House

A 1739 WOOD-SHINGLE FARMHOUSE IN FAIRFIELD

I t took ten years for Serge and Patty Gagarin to acquire the house, but the long wait, they both say, was well worth it. For when they did at last purchase this wood-shingled, 1739 farmhouse in Fairfield, Connecticut, they knew their dreams had been brought to fruition.

The requirements they had established when they began their house search had been simply these: The house must be old and it must be situated well off the road in a bucolic setting. Patty Gagarin quickly discovered three properties that met these requirements, but unfortunately, none was for sale. Ten years later this weathered farmhouse went on the market, and when it did, the Gagarins, of course, purchased it immediately. The old house not only satisfied their requirements perfectly, it also possessed, they felt, a unique quality—"a singularity," as Patty Gagarin describes it—that attracted them both.

The house is indeed possessed of a most singular character, but pinpointing precisely what it is that generates this unique appeal is quite another matter. Certainly, the structure is interesting: this is, after all, a house of eighteenth-century origin that wears the decades nobly. And the furnishings—primitive American antiques of fine caliber—hold promise of absorbing stories to be told. One senses, however, that appealing though they may be, these properties are not what imbue the house with its rare spirit. Perhaps it is simply as Serge Gagarin suggests: what makes this house so inviting is that it is vener-

The house still claims its original front door (LEFT). *It was customary in colonial times to tuck a penny coined during the year the house was built beneath the sill. The penny discovered beneath this sill is dated 1735, but as the owners explain, if the builder lacked a penny dated the year the house was built, he substituted one coined during a year approximately the date of construction.*

Atop the stone wall that borders the herb garden is a small portion of a collection of antique birdhouses and weather vanes (RIGHT).

Added to the property in 1929, a graceful fan gate marks the entrance to the drive (TOP).

The central core of the house (ABOVE) was built by John Banks in 1739; the dining room wing to the left was added in the 1920s; what was once an animal shed to the right, is now a covered patio.

The rear view of the house reveals its rambling layout (RIGHT). At center is the original structure; the three dormer windows were added in 1929. To the left is the covered patio that once stabled livestock; to the right and far right are the kitchen wings.

able in a congenial sort of way. It is impressive without seeming imposing, a bit grand, but welcoming just the same. And though richly endowed with a past, it is perfectly comfortable with the present—a house proud not only of what it has been, but of what it has become as well.

The Gagarins, who both admit to a strong interest in New England history, have long been captivated by Fairfield, a place steeped in New England history and tradition. One of Connecticut's earliest settlements, Fairfield was established in the autumn of 1639 by Roger Ludlow and a small band of adventurous wayfarers. Ludlow had been one of the founders of the Connecticut colony and had come to the spot that would become Fairfield in an endeavor to extend the settlement into the eastern sector of the colony. The area to which Ludlow laid claim was known as Unquowa among the local Pequot Indians—a name that meant "the place beyond" and was fitting for a region to which white settlers had yet to venture.

This eighteenth-century oil painting of a young child with a pet rabbit was executed by the nineteenth-century folk artist Zedekiah Belknap. The original built-in cupboard filled with chalkware was incorporated into the corner of the library at the time the house was built. The continuous-arm braced-back Windsor chairs were crafted by E. B. Tracy during the eighteenth century. The child's chair was a wedding gift.

Although Indian tribes had presented a considerable threat to the settlement of the New England colonies, by 1639 the native Pequot population of the area to which Ludlow laid claim had lost many of its number to the diseases the early European settlers had brought to the region. The Indians were, therefore, unable to mount much resistance to Roger Ludlow's usurpation of their land. The territory Ludlow wrested from the Indians encompassed all of the land extending from Saugatuck River in the west to the Stratford bounds (now Fairfield's Park Avenue) in the east—an area that stretched a distance of roughly twelve miles inland from Long Island Sound.

The founders called their new settlement Fairfield—a name descriptive of the hundreds of acres of rich salt marshes that were developed into bountiful agricultural plots. While much of the settlement was destroyed by the British during the Revolution, and few seventeenth-century dwellings survive in Fairfield today, evidence remains of Roger Ludlow's plan for the town. Post Road, Old Post Road,

In the room the owners refer to as "the big living room," the sofa to the right is an early country sofa that most probably was never upholstered, but rather simply covered with a plain cloth of some type. The covered chair is a make-do chair—a ladderback chair covered in an unpretentious fashion. The upholstered sofa is another country sofa, which was cut down to better suit the scale of the room. The painted chests are of eighteenth-century vintage as is the apothecary chest in the corner, which came from a Connecticut convent. The exposed ceiling beams date the house as pre-1740.

A small, burled pine table in the dining room supports a charming mélange of collectibles—candlesticks, Shaker boxes, and antique weather vanes (LEFT). The chairs flanking the table are eighteenth-century great chairs, which were traditionally reserved for the patriarch of a family.

Beach Road, and South Benson Road form a grid around the Town Green—a grid laid out by Roger Ludlow. It was on these streets that Fairfield's settlers built their homes, their meeting houses, their church, their town hall.

By the time the settlement of Fairfield was approaching its centennial, the town had grown into one of Connecticut's more thriving communities. Among those who had prospered exceptionally well was John Banks, the wealthy farmer who built the house the Gagarins now own. Constructed in 1739, the house encompassed generously proportioned, high-ceilinged rooms, the size and number of which were indicative of John Banks's considerable wealth. The original first floor rooms included the hall, the keeping room, the parlor, the borning room, and an ell at the rear that housed the kitchen. Three bedrooms, two small storage rooms, a hall, and an attic space were above.

While this was never a modest farmhouse—it would have been considered a rather spacious dwelling by the standards of its day—it does exhibit the structural simplicity that distinguished the houses

A spacious but cozy room, the library—or "little living room," as the owners often refer to it—is where friends and family often gather to unwind (RIGHT). The focal point here is the bold red-and-white quilt, one of many antique quilts in the owner's collection. Comfortable sofas upholstered in red-and-white fabrics invite relaxation, and folk-art accessories draw the eye to every corner. The paintings are examples of fine folk-art portraiture by artists of the Prior-Hamblen school. The woman is a Prior, the children portraits are by W. W. Kennedy. The table is an antique country pine piece accessorized with a pair of nineteenth-century toy horses. The pillows, most of which were sewn from antique quilts, complement the hanging quilt.

60

built throughout the New England colonies during the early 1700s. Boxlike in shape and organized in a two-story plan with attic space in the upper reaches, the house is constructed of wood, its beams exposed on the interior. Doors and windows are framed plainly and the structure, in general, exhibits an absence of embellishment. Dormers are incorporated into the rear roofline and the chimney is built into an end wall. The shingled facade is characteristic of many Connecticut colonials.

Fortunately, this structural simplicity was preserved as the house changed ownership through the years and was enlarged to its present size. The house remained much as John Banks built it until the 1920s, having survived the ravages of the Revolution.

When the Revolutionary War broke out during the 1770s, Connecticut was the scene of almost constant battle as soldiers from Brit-

Primitives—furniture, paintings, and quaint, whimsical carvings—are incorporated into the decor of every room. This charming folk-art grouping of antique toys assembled on a library windowsill is one of many such collections found throughout the house.

The dining room, which was added to the house in the 1920s, is a spacious room used for large family gatherings or for formal entertaining. The walls are constructed of old wood that was embellished with a rustic decorative painted finish. The table is an eighteenth-century painted harvest table, as are the dining chairs.

Past and present have been melded in the kitchen, which was designed with an emphasis on convenience but which exudes the cozy feel of the kitchen/keeping rooms of the past (RIGHT). Work space is well zoned so the room can service a good deal of entertaining. Track lighting was chosen to illuminate the work area because the lamps can be quickly and easily directed. Hanging baskets, copper cookware, and dried herbs from the garden contribute to the relaxed atmosphere.

The kitchen sitting and dining area is a gathering spot favored by family and friends—a delightful corner where primitive antiques and collectibles set the stage. The table is an eighteenth-century butch table, the chairs, New London County Windsor chairs circa 1760. A varied sampling of the Gagarins' collection of antique toys is incorporated here, including several nineteenth-century cloth dolls and colorful wooden blocks. Both game boards are intriguing, but the "Sun, Moon, and Stars" board is exceptionally fine and is bequeathed to the American Folk Art Museum. The accent pillows have been made from fragments of antique quilts. Although the room is of new construction, old planks, beams, and bricks were used to augment the colonial style.

The Gagarins converted the original "borning" room into a bar area (BELOW). In addition to the bar itself, the room incorporates a small seating area, often used when the owners dine alone or entertain a small group of friends. The bar was constructed from old planks acquired specifically for that purpose. Beyond is the library.

The stone and brick fireplace (BOTTOM) which successfully hid three revolutionary soldiers in 1779 has been well-preserved and not only provides heat for the big living room but also functions as an appealing structural element. The brick was once used as ballast in eighteenth-century Dutch ships.

ish-controlled Long Island raided the coast. The townspeople of Fairfield were strong supporters of the colonies' fight for independence, and the town's defense was placed in the hands of Gold Selleck Silliman, a former sea captain. In the spring of 1779 Silliman was kidnapped by Tory forces—a plot hatched to prevent him from thwarting a British plan to invade Fairfield County. The Tories' efforts were successful and on July 7, 1779, 2,000 British troops invaded the area. By the time the last troops had departed the following night, most of Fairfield had been burned to the ground.

The British did send a squad to the Banks house in search of revolutionary soldiers, but the search proved fruitless. Mrs. Banks had hidden three soldiers in the smoke box of the main fireplace and, denying to the British any knowledge of the soldiers, continued to prepare dinner in that very fireplace. Although the British fired a cannonball at the house, it was not burned.

In the 1920s the house was sold to a woman who enlarged it by

adding a dining-room wing and expanding the kitchen ell. To ensure the architectural compatibility of the new structures with the existing house, the woman engaged the services of experts from the Metropolitan Museum of Art in New York, which at that time provided consultation and design services to private individuals undertaking the preservation or renovation of historic structures. As a result of the museum's efforts, the structural integrity of the original house was preserved. Although the kitchen has been renovated since, the dining room remains today as it was constructed in the 1920s, speaking clearly and appropriately in the seventeenth-century vernacular.

One of the subsequent owners enlarged the house further by adding a playroom and bath off of the kitchen. The Gagarins have landscaped the grounds, converted a lean-to into a covered patio, and incorporated a number of decorative cosmetic details throughout the house. The most significant changes they have wrought, however, have been in the kitchen. Today, the kitchen encompasses both a spacious work area and a sitting and dining area warmed by a fireplace. The Gagarins made extensive use of old materials—eighteenth-century weathered beams and mellowed panelling, for example—but incorporated such contemporary elements as the track lighting and new tile for convenience.

The Gagarins also converted the original borning room into a cozy bar area, which is frequently used for informal dining and is a spot to which guests seem to flock. The furnishings, of course, have much to do with why people are so drawn to the space. Here, as throughout the house, Patty Gagarin has employed colors and patterns that are exuberant without being contradictory to the colonial simplicity that is clearly the dominant design force. Checked cottons in bright shades of yellow and red harmonize well with the rich tones of the wood in this room and inject a lively splash of color. The amusing folk art and primitives used to accessorize the room add a bit of humorous punctuation.

Patty Gagarin is an antiques dealer with a predilection for primitive furnishings and folk art, and she has furnished the house with a wonderful assortment of such pieces. "Aside from the fact that primitives do possess a special beauty, they are also wonderfully versatile," she says. "You can move them about from room to room—something I do frequently—and achieve new looks quite effortlessly."

Incorporated into the Gagarin house are pieces that are whimsical, quaint, and beautifully simple as well. Antique birdhouses settle together quite comfortably with old baskets, chests, hooked rugs, faded quilts, chalkware, pine tables, and weather vanes of every imaginable configuration. The ambience is relaxed —this is the sort of house that beckons you within and invites you to stay. "I think most people feel naturally a bit more comfortable with rustics and primitives," says Patty Gagarin. "They feel more inclined to sit down and relax, enjoy themselves, not worry about what they're sitting on, or what they've just placed their drink on, or whether they can rub their fingers across a finish of a piece that intrigues them. The ultimate goal for any of us in decorating a home is to create a place where all who enter feel comfortable and welcome. I feel that we have achieved that with this house and it's a very satisfying feeling."

One of the more elegantly furnished rooms in the house is the master bedroom (LEFT). The effect here is soft-edged and soothing—the perfect prescription for dissolving the tensions of the day. The canopy is a piece of decorative sleight-of-hand made simply by gathering fabric and tacking it to the ceiling.

In a bow to modern comfort, a reproduction four-poster was chosen for the guest room (ABOVE). Antique beds are not as ample as those made today; there were no queen- or king-sized beds until fairly recently. The other furnishings in the room, however, are antiques selected to complement the bed's simple styling.

Sabbath Day House

A CONVERTED 1740 MEETING HOUSE IN WOODBURY

In moving the Sabbath Day House (LEFT) from its original site across the street, Ken Hammitt was taking part in a venerable New England tradition. Well into the nineteenth century, houses were routinely moved from their original site and were adapted and renovated for a new owners' uses. Visible here are two of this owner's alterations to the 1740 building: a bedroom wing on the left and the garage on the right.

The original 1740 trim around the front door (RIGHT) is painted a rusty red color that accurately duplicates the shade that would have been used in the eighteenth century. The carved raised panel design gives a pleasing geometric pattern to the front door, which is the eighteenth-century original, as are the sidelights.

Ninety miles from the lively bustle of New York City, Woodbury, Connecticut, is an exquisitely pastoral village that offers a tranquil pace, an unassuming charm, and a history that spans three centuries. Encompassing thirty-seven square miles in southeastern Litchfield County and populated by just slightly more than 7,000 residents, Woodbury is a place to which weekend sojourners from the city often come to poke about in antiques shops or enjoy the brilliant foliage in the autumn.

For anyone with even a slight interest in American architecture, Woodbury is a treat to explore, for the town has a well-preserved architectural legacy of seventeenth-, eighteenth-, and nineteenth-century buildings. Mingling amicably side by side on Woodbury's streets or across neighboring fields are structures of the Colonial, Georgian, Federal, Greek Revival, and Victorian styles as well as the occasional twentieth-century contemporary. Adding to Woodbury's appeal is its informal plan, which, since the town's settlement in 1659, has intermixed residential, agricultural, and commercial areas.

It was to this beautiful Connecticut town that Kenneth Hammitt came in 1953, because it seemed to him an ideal little village in which to take up residence after five years of living and working in England. A writer by profession and an inveterate collector "by some fortune or misfortune," as he puts it, Ken Hammitt gradually abandoned writing in favor of buying and selling antiques—an occupation that satisfies

This arresting collection of small decorative objects includes several English delftware plates dating from the eighteenth century and some choice pieces of brass, including a dainty teapot embellished with the coat of arms of North Carolina (RIGHT).

In *Ken Hammitt's* library, which is filled with his favorite novels and biographies, he has placed a desk that was made by Woodbury, Connecticut, cabinetmaker Elijah Booth around 1780. The Chippendale chair in front of the desk dates from the same period (FAR RIGHT).

70

his appreciation for fine old furniture and decorative objects, even if many of those pieces eventually find their way into the homes of others. It is also, he has found, an occupation that is eminently compatible with his love of old houses.

Ken Hammitt is especially drawn to old buildings in need of repair—an attraction that prompted him to buy the neglected Sabbath Day House on Main Street and convert it into a home for himself and his wife, Barbara, and their young grandson, Alex McCandless.

Built about 1740 as a meeting place where townsfolk could gather between church services, the Sabbath Day House was a simple structure—a small, four-room building designed as little more than basic shelter. "It was hardly what you'd call an architectural treasure," Ken Hammitt recalls. "There really wasn't much to it at all. It was a tiny little place with no heating or plumbing, but because it was falling in I wanted to save it. I felt sorry for it."

Characteristically restrained in design, the building has much in common with the seventeenth- and eighteenth-century farmhouses seen today throughout New England, and adheres to the same aesthetic of clean lines, neat proportions, and straightforward architectural definition. In its simplicity, the meeting house closely resembles the one-and-a-half-story colonial farmhouses built throughout New England in the early-eighteenth century. The second floor of these houses was nestled into the steeply pitched roof and a central chimney provided warmth for both levels, which have two rooms on each floor.

Originally, the structure stood across the road from its present site. The owner had it moved onto property adjoining his antiques shop, a spacious, rather elegant mid-eighteenth-century house that the Hammitts previously occupied. No longer needing—or wanting—a large house, they thought that with some expansion and refurbishment, the Sabbath Day House would make a charming residence.

Because the building was so run-down when Ken Hammitt bought it, many of the original structural elements had to be dis-

71

The view through the original six-over-six paned window (ABOVE) looks out on Ken Hammitt's antiques shop across the drive from the Sabbath Day House on Woodbury's Main Street.

The small dining area on the second floor has a pretty view of the picket-fenced front yard (RIGHT). The 1810 chairs in front of the window were made in New York, as was the large mahogany table in the foreground, which the owner attributes to Duncan Phyfe. Although usually identified with New York City, where the nineteenth-century cabinetmaker had his workshop, Phyfe built a house in the Woodbury area, which explains why furniture attributed to him has been found there.

Poised above the carved wooden folk-art whimsy of a bird is a seventeenth-century brass and iron candleholder. On the wall behind it is an English reflecting mirror made about 1740 (FAR RIGHT).

carded. But wherever feasible, the owners replaced them with old materials salvaged from other buildings. The eighteenth-century oak flooring, for example, was retrieved from a house the owner found being dismantled in Hartford. A few structural compromises were also made—the clapboards on the front of the house are old, but those on the sides are new. The new siding was made to appear old, however, by reversing it so that the rough surface is exposed.

Renovating the house required building a new foundation. Because the new site of the structure is on a slope, the rooms at the front of the first floor are underground, while those at the back look out on the green lawn of the backyard. Building the new foundation allowed Ken Hammitt to expand the house considerably, thus the first floor includes a living room, dining room, library, and kitchen. On the second level, which, because of the sloped site, is entered through the front door, there is a second living room, dining room, and kitchen, two bedrooms and three bathrooms. Tucked under the sloped eaves of the third floor is another bedroom and bathroom.

The furnishings give the restoration its distinctive personality. The furniture is American, the accessories primarily English, and all of the pieces are representative of those Ken Hammitt acquires for his shop. The art, which is American, is a collection of the old and the new. There are paintings by early American painters as well as several by the contemporary artist Peter Poskas, who frequently paints Woodbury scenes.

The owners intentionally designed the rooms to focus the eye on the antique American furniture. The door and mantels are painted with soft blue, green, or drab-colored paints that approximate shades that might have been used in eighteenth-century houses. These backgrounds serve as a perfect foil for the fine period furnishings Ken Hammitt has assembled. There is, for example, the bonnet-top highboy made for General Benjamin Talmadge of Litchfield, Connecticut, an aide to George Washington during the Revolutionary War. The Hammits also have other pieces of furniture made in Connecticut by anonymous colonial cabinetmakers. "Cabinetmakers were very important members of the community in colonial Connecticut," says Ken Hammitt, "but few of them signed their furniture." Frequently self-taught and self-trained, eighteenth-century colonial Connecticut

Several colonial New England pieces of furniture are displayed in the first floor living room, including, on the left, a wing chair that was probably made in Connecticut in the late-eighteenth century and a Massachusetts lowboy cabinet next to it, dating about 1760. Above the barrel-shaped upholstered late-eighteenth-century chair on the right is a recent painting by Peter Poskas, a comtemporary Woodbury artist.

Above the Massachusetts camelback sofa in the second floor living room (TOP LEFT) is a painting by the Woodbury contemporary artist Peter Poskas, whose work the owner collects. The corner chair in the foreground was made in Connecticut in the eighteenth century, as was the cherry wood tea table.

In the downstairs dining area (BOTTOM LEFT) is a circular butch table surrounded by Connecticut Queen Anne chairs. The cupboard against the wall is a mid-eighteenth-century Massachusetts piece, still retaining its original red wash painted finish.

Decorated with a bonnet-top and shell carvings, this highboy is a fine piece of Connecticut colonial cabinetmaking, crafted in Litchfield around 1770. Beside it is one of a pair of continuous arm Windsor chairs, also made in Connecticut. Making a striking showing on the wall is one of a pair of English delftware wallpockets, filled with copper and gold dried flowers (RIGHT).

Standing regally in the corner of one of the bedrooms (LEFT) is a cherry wood linen press that was fashioned in Kent, Connecticut, in the eighteenth century. The airborne deer over the French doors is a weathervane made in Salisbury, Massachusetts, in the nineteenth century.

In the cozy guest room nestled under the third floor eaves (RIGHT) are displayed a Connecticut-made Windsor chair and a desk, primarily of cherry wood, which were crafted by the eighteenth-century Woodbury, Connecticut, cabinetmaker Elijah Booth. The desk is embellished with a Masonic emblem.

Gazing up the stairway to the third floor is a menagerie of American carved wooden folk-art animals made in the eighteenth and nineteenth centuries (ABOVE).

A nineteenth-century duck decoy sits pertly on a crossbeam near an eighteenth-century Windsor chair in the bathroom (RIGHT).

cabinetmakers most often used cherry wood and improvised designs of their own. As a result, says Ken Hammitt, colonial Connecticut furniture can be "rather wild." That wildness may take the form of carved details or an overall design that is more idiosyncratic than a piece fashioned in an urban area would be.

Gifted with a discerning eye for design, Ken Hammitt has put his furniture into arrangements in which different decades and styles blend harmoniously. This approach is a traditional New England one. "Our forebears never went out and bought themselves perfectly matched sets of furniture," he says. "There were sets of dining chairs, of course, but then, too, people often had mismatched chairs around

the table. And they spent their lifetimes accumulating furniture. Only occasionally did they get rid of something, and that was when it wore out, fell apart, or was needed more by a relative or friend. All of this accumulation was passed along to the next generation, who went about furnishing their homes in very much the same way—save for what they might have inherited, which was always somehow worked in." The furniture Ken Hammitt has assembled testifies to the skill and inventiveness of the colonial cabinetmakers. And the house he rescued has become a thoroughly appropriate environment in which to display and enjoy these fine pieces of the early New England cabinetmakers' artistry.

Thomas Buckingham House

A CONTEMPORARY RENOVATION OF A 1785 MARITIME HOUSE IN ESSEX

Built about 1785, the Thomas Buckingham House (LEFT) is a country farmhouse constructed on a four-room over four-room plan. In rural colonial New England, it was not unusual for styles to lag a generation or two, or for elements of earlier styles to be intermixed with the latest architectural fashion. That explains why this house has an early feature—a center chimney instead of the later Georgian double chimney.

A semi-octagonal bay dining room, visible to the right, and a screened porch were added to the house in the 1930s (RIGHT).

People are drawn to New England colonial houses for many reasons. They like living in a place that has a tie to the past; they take pleasure in the solid old construction, the mellow antique woodwork, and the signs of handwork. For people who love colonial houses, there is no question that they would rather not live in any other kind of house.

For just those reasons, when Jim and Audrey Simon decided to leave New York City and buy a house in Essex, Connecticut, they knew they wanted an authentic colonial. The house they found was a country farmhouse built around 1785, fifty feet above the edge of the Connecticut River. The river bends around the house, and a ferry once operated off the tip of land nearby. Town records are not clear as to when the house was built, but they do indicate that in 1785 the property was owned by Thomas Buckingham, whose descendents continued to own the land well into the 1800s. Tradition holds that Thomas Buckingham was a shipbuilder, which is very probable since Essex was a busy port town in a state where shipbuilding was a backyard industry in colonial times. There is also evidence of Thomas Buckingham's profession in the house—a ship's mast that runs from the cellar straight up to the attic, serving the center post of the spiral staircase.

Built in a four-room over four-room plan with a center hall, the house is straightforward in its design. All the windows casings are flat.

The semi-octagonal bay added to the dining room in the 1930s has a second story balcony (ABOVE). This view was taken from the balcony, looking toward the cupola on the garage.

The addition (BELOW) was designed by the present owners to relate to the original eighteenth-century farmhouse, on the right. The two sections are joined by galleries that feature full-height mullioned windows on the first floor. For the addition, on the left, owner-architect Jim Simon designed an outside chimney wall of granite and brick, mullioned windows, and clean-lined gables—all colonial style elements—to unify the new section of the house with the 1780s core.

Furnished with a new natural wicker settee and chair, the porch offers a tranquil spot to relax on a summer day (RIGHT). The cushions were made by the owner with Laura Ashley fabric. The wrought iron base of the coffee table is a junkyard find transformed with the addition of a glass top. A garden of potted plants is displayed on an iron baker's rack.

Right off the small entrance hall a spiral stairway leads up to the second story. House legend says that the support post running up the stairwall is a ship's mast, built into the house from the cellar clear up to the attic. The wide-board pine floors are original. The small chest beneath the wrought iron mirror is probably a spice or apothecary chest from the early-nineteenth century.

Comfortable seating is assured by the presence of the oversized sofa in the living room (ABOVE). The scrubbed pine table before the sofa was once a desk; it was cut down for its present role as a generous-sized coffee table.

There are no moldings nor are there any of the architectural carvings and trims that can be seen in the more formal 1780s houses within the village of Essex. Situated just outside the village, this unpretentious house may have been connected with the ferry business that once operated nearby. There was certainly a farm on the property, which was once a large piece of land running right down to the Connecticut River.

Although the land has been subdivided over the years, the house has remained intact. Various twentieth-century owners treated the original house as a core onto which they built additions. During the 1930s, a porch was built on one side of the house and a one-story addition was attached to the other side. Three decades later, a second

story was built on top of the 1930s ground floor addition. When the Simons bought the house in 1985 they embarked on a renovation plan of their own that preserved the main core of the house while restructuring the house to create the spaces they needed.

An architect by profession with his own firm in New Haven, Jim Simon reworked the 1930s–1960s remodel to give the exterior a more gracious appearance and gain the larger kitchen and master bedroom the couple wanted. The old two-story addition was completely gutted. On the first floor a spacious modern kitchen was installed, and upstairs the new master bedroom was created. To connect this section to the original part of the house Jim Simon designed gallery-like halls that are pierced with light-giving windows. The exterior of the two-

The bay window in the dining room looks out on the springtime backyard greenery. The bowback Windsor chairs are reproductions that the owner finished with a dark stain to match the nineteenth-century pine wine-tasting table. The placemats were crocheted by the owner's great-grandmother.

In the windowed corridor that connects the original house to the newly added wing, a stripped pine cupboard shows off a collection of flower-sprigged plates. The view is through the dining room to the living room (ABOVE).

By the 1780s the panelled chimney breast that had been common early in the century had disappeared and small fireplaces topped with mantels, like the one in this dining room, became a more favored design. The postage stamp quilt above the drop-leaf pine table is part of the owner's collection of early American quilts (RIGHT).

story addition was completely reworked to create an appearance that is sympathetic with the old section of the house. Like the original section, it is sheathed in clapboard siding. The colonial-style mullioned windows that were installed in the addition also serve as unifying elements. Since this end of the house has the best views of the river, the owners wanted to be sure to capitalize on them. Exercising his creative license the architect designed vigorous gabled peaks on the exterior of the second story addition, forming a subtle reference to traditional American residential architecture, and uniting the original colonial section with the new living quarters.

Future renovation plans will eventually include the rehabilitation of a charming cottage on the property to use as a studio and guest

On a trip to England the owners found this large antique combination bookcase and cabinet of stripped pine. It fits the den so well that it could have been custom built for the room. The bookcase and cabinet, the modular couch, and the Laura Ashley pillows and wallpaper create a successful mix of modern design and country colonial style. The batten board cabinet built high up in the wall is called a parsons box. Set against the chimney wall, it was used to keep food warm in colonial times (ABOVE).

In the new kitchen addition (RIGHT), the custom-made cabinets meld traditional and contemporary elements. Overall, their look is crisp and modern. The detailing, however, depends on traditional forms—glass-paned cabinets above, raised panel cabinets below. The counters are butcher-block and the handmade octagonal tiles are from Mexico.

In the newly added master bedroom, the
gabled roof creates an intriguing series of
angles in the ceiling. Since the ceiling height
is quite low in the colonial part of the
house, the owners decided to design a
vaulted ceiling on the new second floor to
give the bedroom a sense of soaring height.
Against the intense sapphire blue walls, the
shape of the ceiling is dramatically emphasized by contrasting white paint. The
room's traditional detailing—mullioned
windows, simple granite fireplace, and raised
panel closet doors—subtly refer back to the
eighteenth-century farmhouse core.

Beneath the gables of the new master bedroom is a cozy window seat (ABOVE). The small square-windowed alcove above it is poised in the very peak of the gable to let in light and create a play of solid and void.

From the window of this second floor guest bedroom (RIGHT), it is possible to get a bird's-eye view over the Connecticut River in wintertime. The curved-arm chair is a Lincoln rocker that was in Audrey Simon's family.

house. Once probably a lean-to kitchen attached to the back of the house, the structure was moved and turned into a separate dwelling in the 1930s. Unheated, it must have served then as a summer guest cottage. Today, it creates a picturesque vignette on the property, especially in the spring when the apple trees and dogwoods that surround it are in full blossom.

Inside the main house, the Simons have furnished the rooms with a mixture of possessions from their single days, furniture passed along by their families, and a few carefully chosen new acquisitions. Stripped pine British cupboards, reproduction Windsor chairs, antique tables, and refreshing accents of contemporary wicker furniture fill the rooms. Here and there are the colorful counterpoints provided by Audrey Simon's collection of quilts, which hang on walls and drape across chairs and beds. The look is casual and energetic, with a bow to the past. This blend of old and new is perfect for the new spirit that the owners have brought to the Thomas Buckingham House.

The vanity in the master bathroom (LEFT) is a nineteenth-century pine washstand that has been outfitted with double oval sinks and a new counter of Chiampo Rosa marble.

Captain Amos Palmer House

A PRIVATEER'S ELEGANT 1787 TOWN HOUSE IN STONINGTON

The gardens at the rear of the house (LEFT) are a profusion of blossoms three seasons out of the year. Following the designs of English eighteenth-century gardens, the owner created the raised flower beds framed by broad pebble walks. The entire design is offset by boxwood hedges, a favored evergreen in English formal gardens of the eighteenth century.

Although it was reconstructed after the War of 1812, the Captain Amos Palmer House retains its handsome colonial exterior. The front door (RIGHT), flanked by broad pilasters and topped by a simple entablature, is a fine example of colonial woodwork. Beneath the steps is a door leading to a ground floor space that was an apothecary shop in the nineteenth century.

L ooking out on the harbor of Stonington, which edges on the blue waters of Long Island Sound, the Captain Amos Palmer House has a past steeped in American history.

Captain Amos Palmer, who built the house in 1787, was a loyal privateer. During the Revolution, privateering became an effective weapon against the English. Hundreds of privately owned American vessels, idled because of the disruption of American maritime trade, were commissioned by the Continental Congress and the states to menace the British. While the small American navy had no hope of challenging the large and well-equipped British naval fleet, the plucky privateers picked away at the British merchant marine, capturing her cargo-laden frigates and crippling Britain's trade. With seaports fringing the coastline, Connecticut actively supported loyal privateering, commissioning during the course of the Revolution 300 privateer vessels, which captured some 500 British merchant marine ships and their cargos. Half this seized booty went to Connecticut, the rest was split among the privateer's owners, captain, and crew. The spoils of privateering built many fine captains' houses throughout eighteenth-century New England, including the Amos Palmer House.

Constructed against a hillock on the foundation of a house that had been destroyed by fire, the Amos Palmer House was designed in a large two-and-a-half story five-room over five-room plan with a central chimney. This traditional design with a clapboard exterior is

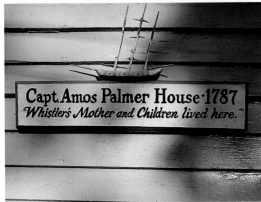

Capt. Amos Palmer House · 1787
Whistler's Mother and Children lived here.

The living room's fine fireplace wall woodwork probably dates from 1787 (TOP). In the late 1930s previous owners added the bow windows. They also exposed the hand-hewn beams and stained them a dark wood color; the present owners painted them white. The Martha Washington armchair near the fireplace is a centennial piece, made in the late-nineteenth century. The term "centennial" refers to objects made after 1876 when the celebration of America's first hundred years created a popular national trend for colonial style furniture.

The frigate above the house name (ABOVE) refers to the privateer vessel captained by Amos Palmer, who made his fortune as a loyal privateer during the Revolutionary War.

Seen against the window's light is a model of the three-masted Falcon, which sailed out of New Bedford, Massachusetts, in the nineteenth century (RIGHT).

Above the fireplace in the living room are an eighteenth-century flintlock musket and a powder horn used in the French and Indian Wars. The gilt mirror is embellished with an eagle, a favored emblem of American Federal period design (FAR RIGHT).

96

known as the central chimney Cape. After the house was fired on in the British attack on Stonington during the War of 1812, its interior was reconstructed in its present form, a central-hallway Federal style.

The story of that British attack deserves telling since Amos Palmer and his house played a colorful part in it. On August 9th, 1814, four British ships anchored off Stonington and demanded surrender of the town or they would begin their attack within one hour. Citizens lit warning fires on Tar Barrel Hill and started evacuating women and children. This distress call brought in volunteer troops from nearby towns, and powder and ball which was sorely needed.

The bombardment began in the evening. Two heavy eighteen-pounder cannon were already at the small battery on the point and drove the British from the harbor, causing them to round the point in darkness and renew their attack at sunrise from Little Narragansett Bay on the eastern side. The Amos Palmer House, set high on the knoll, was a particular target of British cannon fire and suffered a number of direct hits before the ships were driven off by the small but accurate Stonington shore battery.

In an eyewitness account written from his house, Captain Amos Palmer estimated that, in all, the British shelled Stonington with sixty tons of metal. Many of those cannonballs fell on the captain's own house. The first ball made a direct hit through the roof and took down the central chimney. A second ball hit a stone wall, shattering all of the windows on the south side of the house. Finally, when a British cannonball was vollied through the back door and burst right through the front door, Amos Palmer had had enough. The story

Dating from many periods and including an array of
styles, the owners' collection of furniture includes this
Victorian settee that was in the 1876 trousseau of Alice
Houston's great-grandmother. The pewter sconce above it
was installed by previous owners of the house in 1938.

The table at the top of the stairs is an 1840 Shaker sewing table from Enfield, New Hampshire, which descended down through Alice Houston's family.

The brilliant yellow color of the front hallway (LEFT) was chosen by the owners because it is one of the colors most frequently used in Federal period interiors. The lowboy near the front door is an eighteenth-century piece.

The owners made the dining table themselves, following the style of a colonial trestle table they had seen in the Metropolitan Museum of Art in New York City. The antique wideboard planks that form the table top were used in nineteenth-century farmhouse noonings, during which they would be unfolded outdoors and set for lunch for the farm hands. Around the table are nineteenth-century American ladderback chairs. The seventeenth-century brass chandelier from the Houston house in Scotland, is Dutch (FAR LEFT).

A collection of American and English pewter ware is arranged in the plate rack on the dining room wall (LEFT).

An eighteenth-century Northern Italian painting hangs above the Sheraton sideboard. The knifebox came down through James Houston's family (ABOVE).

The portrait above the English highboy in the living room (ABOVE) is of a Scottish member of the family. Alice Houston created the crewel embroidery on the Queen Anne-style chairs.

The owners' nickname for the color in the living room is "Independence Hall gray"; they decided on the color after a visit to Independence Hall, where the walls are the same silvery tone. The focal point in the living room is the Queen Anne table, which the owners believe was crafted by the Goddard Townsend families of cabinetmakers in Rhode Island. The maple desk near the windows is from Connecticut (RIGHT).

goes that when the iron ball cooled off, the captain picked it up in his hat, hurried down to the battery, and gave it to the Connecticut militia men to return to the British, with his compliments. The militia loaded the cannonball into one of the eighteen-pound cannons marshaled in Stonington's defense and fired it straight into a British barge. Seeing the strike, the avenged Captain Palmer turned on his heel and headed home.

In rebuilding the house, Amos Palmer retained its colonial appearance on the outside. The graceful slope of the Georgian roof was repaired, and the front and back doors were designed to replace those destroyed by cannon fire. The front door is a particularly handsome example of colonial woodwork, with its broad pilasters at the sides and sculptural, almost wedge-shaped cornice on the entablature

above the door. Most of the exterior parts of the house, however, were updated in the Federal style that had become fashionable in the early 1800s. Although the handsome raised-panel chimney breast in the parlor is a characteristically Georgian finish, the curving staircase and the arches with fine molding in the upstairs and downstairs halls are flourishes of the Federal style.

In the middle of the nineteenth-century, the Whistlers, relatives of the Palmers, occupied this house. Mrs. Whistler, immortalized by her son, James McNeill Whistler, in his famous painting, *Arrangement in Gray and Black No. 1: Portrait of the Painter's Mother*, was the wife of Major George Washington Whistler, a West Point engineer in charge of building the railroad from Providence to Stonington.

The only major structural changes undertaken in the house oc-

curred in 1938 when the wall between the front and back parlor was removed to create one large sitting room, and the two large bow windows to the garden were installed. Probably at this time the overhead beams in the sitting room were exposed, presumably to give the room the hand-hewn colonial look of a keeping room. In the late 1930s and throughout the 1940s American homeowners became captivated by the Colonial Revival that inspired many alterations, not always accurate. Woodwork was "taken down" to what was assumed to be the original raw pine surface, a process that inadvertently destroyed many original painted finishes. And in many houses, plaster ceilings were removed to expose the beams. Today it would be understood that, in the 1800s, in an elegant Federal house like Amos Palmer's, the parlor beams would have been concealed with a plaster finish, not exposed.

103

In 1939, the American Pulitzer-prize winning poet Stephen Vincent Benét, of John Brown's body fame, bought the house.

The present owners of the Captain Amos Palmer House, James and Alice Houston, purchased it from the Benét family in 1983. Charmed by the view of Stonington harbor and the history of the house, the couple were also attracted by the fine structural condition and generous layout. The Houstons have enhanced the outside appearance by designing a backyard garden of raised beds connected by pebbled pathways. The garden blooms for three seasons, with spring bulbs giving way to summer roses and day lilies, which usher in the chrysanthemums of fall.

Inside the house, the owners have made only minor alterations, updating the kitchen and bathrooms and adding bookcases to create a library-sitting room. They have furnished the rooms in a lively mixture of colonial and Victorian antiques and some twentieth-century reproductions. The furniture was gathered over the years from their families and from antiques shops they frequented when they lived in the rambling Rhode Island farmhouse they previously owned. In the rooms of the house that Captain Amos Palmer built, all of it fits comfortably together.

Throughout the house the couple have kept wall colors subdued. To create the colonial look they favor, they have painted most rooms white and highlighted woodwork with accent colors. In this bedroom (LEFT), the original gun-stock support posts in the corners are painted green. The curtains are made from a cotton print by Waverly that features a design borrowed from early American stencils. The turn-posted bed (one of a pair) is probably nineteenth-century.

The four-poster bed (BELOW) looks like an authentic antique, but it was actually made from a Cohasset Colonials kit by James Houston. The lacey tester was made by an Appalachian craftswoman to Alice Houston's specifications. The blanket box at the foot of the bed is a sailor's chest.

By house tradition this sunny corner bedroom (RIGHT) is called Whistler's Mother's Room, for she once lived in the house. The woolwinder near the window is a Canadian antique.

RHODE ISLAND

An Icelandic legend holds that Norwegian navigator Leif Ericsson sailed westward across the Atlantic around AD 1000 and reached the North American mainland. This he named Vinland, supposedly because of the many grape vines he found there. Where he landed can only be speculated; New England, Newfoundland, and Labrador have all been suggested. Some historians are convinced that an ancient tower in Newport, Rhode Island, was erected by the early adventurer, which would have made Ericsson the first European to have reached Rhode Island's shores.

More authenticated is the arrival of Roger Williams in the seventeenth century. In 1635 the Puritan leaders of the Massachusetts Bay Colony issued an order of banishment to one of their citizens. "Whereas Mr. Roger Williams, one of the elders of the Church of Salem, hath broached and divulged new and dangerous opinions against the authority of magistrates; hath also writ letters of defamation, both of magistrates and churches here . . . it is therefore ordered that the said Mr. Williams shall depart out of this jurisdiction . . . not to return any more without license from the Court." Roger Williams did leave his parish in Salem, and headed for the relatively unexplored territory south of Massachusetts. Reaching Narragansett Bay he established a settlement based on the novel idea of unequivocal religious freedom, and "having sense of God's merciful providence upon me," he named the settlement Providence. Purchasing large tracts of land from the Narraganset Indians, Providence became Rhode Island's first town in 1636. It was followed by Newport in 1639, Portsmouth in 1640 (these two towns were united the same year by William Coddington, another religious dissenter from the Massachusetts Bay Colony), and Warwick in 1643. The four towns, combined under the name of Rhode Island and the Providence Plantations, were granted a royal charter by Charles II in 1663.

The dwellings of these early colonists were primative and medieval in style. Rhode Island did, however, produce a distinctive version of the New England house—the Rhode Island stone-ender, its form apparently based on cottages found in Sussex and Wales. Allen G. Noble describes this type of house in *Wood, Brick, & Stone:* "In its most basic form, the Rhode Island stone-ender had one timber-framed chamber affixed to a massive stone gable containing a fireplace and chimney." Very few of these houses survived King Philip's War, which raged between the Indians and colonists around

1675, and most of those that did have been added to and altered.

By the 1700s many of the Rhode Island colonists had turned to sea trade, which they found more profitable than subsistence farming. Newport was the most flourishing town, plying the three-way molasses, rum, slave trade between the West Indies, New England, and Africa. Newport's mercantile ships brought salt from the Mediterranean, logwood from the Honduras, and shipped hemp, fish, lumbers, rice, flour, flaxseed, and candles. From England, Portugal, and the Orient, they brought furniture, china, and luxury goods. They traded with England's enemies, France and Spain, but were not above privateering against French and Spanish ships. Newport's fine harbor and surroundings attracted settlers of every religious persuasion: Quakers, Congregationalists, Anglicans, Anabaptists, Presbyterians, and Independents. The inhabitants became wealthy as merchants, shipbuilders, or suppliers to the seafaring commerce. Fine houses were built by these merchant princes whom Governor-General of the Dominion of New England, Sir Edmund Andros dubbed "the Quaker Grandees." Not permitted to wear grand clothes, many Quakers dressed their houses instead, displaying silver and even gold on their dressers "such as the Queen did not own."

During the eighteenth century, Newport produced two architects of note. From the beginning of the century until 1740 is considered Newport's most brilliant period of building, due in part to self-dubbed "housewright" Richard Munday, who was responsible for Trinity Church, the Sabbatarian Meeting House, and the Colony House, as well as private houses. The later decades owed much to Newport's gifted amateur architect Peter Harrison, who was influenced by many European style books that gradually found their way to the New World. His library was known to include Colin Campbell's *Vitruvius Britannicus*, Hoppu's *Palladio*, Ware's *Designs of Inigo and Others*, and Gibb's two publications *The Book of Architecture* and *Rules for Drawing*. Harrison was responsible for the Redwood Library, the Brick Market, and the Jewish Synagogue, now a national shrine.

Newport's lead over other Rhode Island towns came to an end during the Revolutionary War, when in 1776 the British fleet took over the town until 1779. Over 300 houses were destroyed. The town was slow to recover, and from then on Providence, almost unaffected by the war, took the ascent. Providence's great years were due to the spermaceti candlemaking business controlled by the successful Brown family.

The houses owned by these wealthy families in Rhode Island featured such grandiose details as circular staircases, panelled walls, marble fireplaces, gilded cornices, and mahogany doors. Each town could boast its own fine cabinetmakers who might base their designs on published books such as *The Gentleman's and Builder's Companion* (1739) by William Jones, *The City and County Builders' and Workmen's Treasury of Designs* (1740) by Batty and Thomas Langley, or *The Gentleman's and Cabinet Maker's Director* by Thomas Chippendale, which contained "Designs for Chimney pieces, Lanthorns and Chandeliers, for Halls and Staircases. Likewise various Designs of Household Furniture, both useful and ornamental." The Goddard-Townsend family, famous for several decades as skilled joiners and cabinetmakers, operated from Newport. Henry Bull, who worked in the early-eighteenth century, and Ezekiel Burroughs, at mid-century, were both joiners of repute in the same town, as was John Cahoon, who sold furniture to the wealthy planters of the West Indies between 1748 and 1760. John Carlisle, a descendant of Paul Revere, was a well enough known furniture maker to be painted by Gilbert Stuart.

Not all the houses were on this scale, however. Humble two-room houses with central chimneys still existed in the eighteenth century, but seen more often were the more substantial five-room plan house with upstairs rooms, and some sort of embellishment, molding or carving, decorated the downstairs parlors. Most humble houses would be colored dull red, the paint made from red earth, lamp black, or sour milk. Fancier houses got fancier colors, but by the end of the nineteenth century colors became subdued, for Henry James described Newport's small houses as "little old gray ladies," which he presumed gave a quaint eighteenth-century air to the town.

Rhode Island's colonial dwellings can perhaps best be summed up by a Frenchman, Claude Blanchard of the Commissary Department: "In many houses there are carpets, even upon the stairs. They are very choice in cups and vases for holding tea or coffee, in glasses and decanters and other matters of this kind in habitual use. . . . In general, the houses are very pleasant and kept with extreme neatness, with the mechanic and the countryman, as well as the merchant and the general. In fact their education is very nearly the same. . . . The inhabitants of the entire country are proprietors. They till the earth and drive their own oxen themselves."

Joseph Reynolds House

A THREE-STORY 1695 RED CLAPBOARD IN BRISTOL

In obtaining historic landmark designation for the house (LEFT), which is now a National Historic Landmark, the owners used 1695 as the building date. Some architectural historians believe Joseph Reynolds may have built the house a few years earlier, but there are no written records to prove it. The original double door at the front of the house was replaced at some point in the early 1800s with this pediment-crowned Federal doorway.

When the house was built in the 1690s, it was three stories high with a much steeper pitched roof. The slanted saltbox roof, apparent in this side view (RIGHT), was caused by a later alteration in which the roof was lowered. Extending from the house is the ell, a back wing which once contained the summer kitchen.

Dating from around 1695, the Joseph Reynolds House, or Willowmere as it was called originally, is the oldest surviving three-story colonial house in New England. Designated a National Historic Landmark, the house is significant as a specimen of transitional architecture. Caught at an architectural brink, Willowmere has earmarks of early colonial medievally-derived building techniques, as well as signs of the Georgian style the 1700s would usher in.

Constructed by Joseph Reynolds as a country manor outside of the harbor town of Bristol, the house is built on land his father, Nathanial, was awarded for his heroism in 1676 in King Philip's War. Bristol was a colonial real-estate development, founded by men from the Massachusetts Bay Colony who wanted to create a coastal trading port. In gratitude for the role that the Boston-born Nathanial Reynolds played in helping to vanquish the Narraganset Indians, the proprietors of Bristol awarded him thirty-one acres of land in 1680—one acre in town at the harbor front and thirty acres in what was called out-of-town, in the rural area then known as Bristol Neck.

This town-and-country division of land followed the customary colonial New England practice by which landowners of a settlement held land both in the village, where they usually lived, and in the nearby countryside, where they farmed. The Reynolds family seems to have had a knack for real estate. Soon after he arrived in the colo-

A stunning architectural feature, the staircase (LEFT) is an example of Jacobean era joinery, which still depended on medieval building techniques. The squat turned balusters are typical in form of very early-eighteenth-century staircases, but the thicker, stouter character of the woodwork marks it as seventeenth-century. The owners believe the stairs to be made of chestnut.

nies from England, Nathanial Reynolds's father developed substantial real-estate interests in Boston, eventually owning most of what is now Milk Street. In Rhode Island, the names of generations of Reynolds descendants appear on historic land maps after the 1690s, demonstrating a pattern of land purchases and sales that suggest active real-estate speculating.

Nathanial Reynolds used his harbor front real-estate prize to build a town house for himself in Bristol. Joseph, his son, fulfilled apparent country squire ambitions by building Willowmere and, once it was completed, moving to it twenty members of the Reynolds family. Remarkably, his descendants would own the house continuously until the 1930s.

Clearly designed to accommodate a large family, the house originally had a main three-story section, with a two-story ell, or back wing, attached. At some unknown date after it was built, the original, steeply pitched roof of the main section was lowered and most of the fourth floor attic space disappeared. The house provided plenty of space for many Reynoldses. In the main section of the house seven bedrooms were laid out on the third floor, with another four bedrooms on the second floor. The ground floor was divided into four rooms, including a keeping room and a parlor. The ell contained a summer kitchen and two other rooms on the first floor and a second story sleeping loft.

The central hall, double chimney design of the main section is typical of many late-seventeenth-century colonial New England houses. But the generous proportions and comparatively high ceilings

The spacious character of the stair hall (LEFT) foreshadows the generous proportions and higher ceilings that Georgian architecture would introduce to the colonial New England home. The portraits in the hall and stairwell depict the nineteenth-century descendants of Joseph Reynolds, who built the house.

Converted into the dining room in the 1820s, this was originally the great room. The original fireplace, which would have been massive with the cavernous opening typical of seventeenth-century colonial New England houses, was replaced in 1829 with this much small fireplace and pine mantel (RIGHT).

The owners call this the "Lean-to," but it was probably originally called the cabinet room. Built just behind the keeping room, it is the seventeenth-century version of the present-day study.

The thick, dimensional quality of the carving in the keeping room is seventeenth-century in character. It is a form called "bolection" and is found in the finer houses of this period. Panelling covering the entire wall continued in a simpler form throughout the Georgian period. The strongly colored paint is a twentieth-century attempt to recreate the 1690s marbleized painted finish, which originally covered the entire room. Afternoon tea is set up on an eighteenth-century wine table (LEFT).

of the rooms on the first and second floors foreshadow the spacious rooms of the eighteenth-century Georgian style. The central staircase running three full stories, with a fourth string up into the attic, is a notable example of fully evolved late-medieval English construction, and is thought to be one of the finest surviving early staircases in New England. Both the staircase detailing and the carved, raised panelling in the original keeping room and keeping room chamber belong to late-Jacobean and Christopher Wren English tradition. The marbleized painted finish that still survives on part of the panelling in the keeping room chamber is also a late-seventeenth- and early-eighteenth-century design element.

When Richard and Wendy Anderson, the present owners, bought the house in 1981, it needed repair and maintenance. The couple refurbished the roof and reinforced the whole house with a forest of lollycolumns in the basement. Although the house had had no major structural alterations, it had suffered the wear of time and the misjudgments of past residents. Recent owners had decorated some of the rooms with brightly colored stencils, which, to English-

The richly grained marbleized paintwork on the mantel, applied in the 1690s, was a feature used in finer late-seventeenth- and early-eighteenth-century New England houses. Originally the keeping room chamber, this is the room that Lafayette used when he stayed at the house during the Revolutionary War. The red and white stencilling on the fireplace board is a modern conceit, applied by previous owners, but it is a vibrant complement to the nineteenth-century Ohio eagle quilt. The present owners now use the room as a bedroom (ABOVE).

The low ceiling height of this third floor bedroom is a typical third story treatment (RIGHT). The exposed corner post and beams demonstrate the characteristic straightforward construction of seventeenth-century New England houses.

born Wendy Anderson's eye, seemed incompatible with the house's sophisticated Jacobean country manor interiors. The stencils were easy to conceal, but correcting other changes will be more complicated and costly. Such improvements might include raising the attic roof to the original steep roof-pitch, a restoration the couple is presently considering. They also hope to restore someday the marbleized painted finish in the original keeping room ruined by smoke damage in a fire in 1976. Although the carved panelling in that room was restored by following Historic American Buildings Survey (HABS) drawings made in the 1930s, the marbleizing has yet to be re-created.

Owning the Joseph Reynolds House has prompted Wendy Anderson to delve into the history of the house and the Reynolds family, whom she speaks of with the familiarity of next-door neighbors. She has become a collector of Reynolds family stories, and one of her favorites concerns the Marquis de Lafayette, who, for a short time during the Revolutionary War, turned the house into a command post and residence.

The story goes that the wife of Joseph Reynolds III had been told to expect Lafayette on a September day in 1778. It seems that sometime before the appointed hour a young Frenchman arrived at the house on horseback, tied his mount to a tree in the yard, and, following a perfunctory greeting by Mrs. Reynolds, politely inquired if he might have something to eat. The ever-gracious Mrs. Reynolds generously obliged, seating him at the table she had set for General Lafayette. The young Frenchman, however, was in no apparent hurry and lingered leisurely over his meal. Mrs. Reynolds, nervously anticipating Lafayette's arrival at any moment and concerned that the youth's presence at the table might constitute a breach of decorum, felt compelled to request him to leave. "But, madame, I *am* the marquis," the bemused general told his astonished hostess, who had no idea that the French military leader was a young man of twenty-one.

A more recently discovered feature of the old house is not mentioned in historic records or lore—the ghostly presence, or presences, in the bedroom in the back ell. Wendy and Richard Anderson have not encountered this presence in person. But friends have seen "something" and even captured a bit of it—whatever *it* is—in a photograph. The couple has noticed that pictures inexplicably fall off walls. And things do vanish, only to turn up later in odd places. If there is a ghostly spirit or two, it can only add to what is already an intriguing accumulation of history and legend surrounding the house, which is indisputably one of Rhode Island's notable early colonial architectural relics.

The bathroom (LEFT) is an early-twentieth-century conversion, apparent from the vintage porcelain bathtub that was installed at the time. The stripped pine dresser was crafted in the nineteenth century and is English.

Seen through the doorway (RIGHT) is one of the bedrooms in the ell at the back of the house. The hefty beams and posts of the door evince the solidness of early colonial New England construction.

Vernon House

A 1758 HIGH-STYLE GEORGIAN TOWN HOUSE IN NEWPORT

Although Vernon house (LEFT) bears the name of its second owner and his descendants who lived in it for a century, it is imbued with the personality of Metcalf Bowler, the prosperous merchant who built it in 1758. Showing off his new wealth and fashionable taste, he built his town house in the symmetrical, well-proportioned Georgian style.

The fine quality of the rusticated exterior finish is apparent in this closeup view of the back of the house (RIGHT). Note how groovings have been cut vertically and diagonally above the window on the left, giving the appearance of actual voussoirs, the stone wedge-shaped sections in an arch.

L ook at Newport harbor on a summer day and the scene is a weekend sailor's fancy: sailboats of every type are moored at the water's edge, and as far as the eye can see into the blueness, white sails dot the horizon.

Imagine the same harbor view in the 1750s when Newport was one of the busiest ports in colonial New England. Along the harbor front, the wharves and docks swarmed with activity as merchant ships arrived and departed. To the Caribbean they took horses, building lumber, beef, pork, and other commodities. They returned laden with rum, molasses, and other delicacies, which they traded with the rest of the colonies as far south as the Carolinas.

The dramatic growth of Newport's sea trade in the eighteenth century brought prosperity and new industries. Tanners, ropemakers, and shipping-related tradesmen joined in the commercial din along the harbor. Merchant businesses thrived. The cosmopolitan spirit of the busy seaport was reflected in an eclectic population. Wealthy men from Virginia and the West Indies were as drawn to Newport as Irish servants, Portuguese sailors, and English artisans.

It was a fluid society, where money, resourcefulness, and a show of style could gain one entrance. Newport tastes were sophisticated. The fine-grained mahogany, exotic spices, and other luxuries the merchant ships brought from the Caribbean and other foreign ports were consumed by an affluent society with increasingly genteel aspirations.

The Oriental style frescoed panels in one of the front parlors, now used as a den, may have been painted by a Western artist between 1720 and 1730. Uncovered by workmen making repairs in the 1930s, they had been concealed since the eighteenth century. One reason they were hidden might have been their unsavory subject matter: one panel (RIGHT) shows a person being impaled, another depicts a swimmer being showered with arrows. The peach silk upholstery of the Louis XIII armchairs is a pungent contrast against the black panels and mustard-yellow walls.

The owner often does paperwork at the reproduction Georgian desk her father once owned (LEFT). On the desk is her grandmother's Chinese cinnabar lamp, dressed with the fluted lampshade her grandmother had made in the 1920s.

One mark of this society's taste was the cultivation of its own school of cabinetmaking, centered around the intermarried Townsend-Goddard cabinetmaker family. Working in the close-grained rich mahogany imported from the Caribbean, the Townsend-Goddard cabinetmakers created side tables, chairs, and desks in an elegant style that came to be associated uniquely with Newport.

Elegant architecture was another hallmark of Newport sophistication in the eighteenth century. Here, too, the town's craftsmen developed a dramatic style that was very much Newport's own. Writing about the town's eighteenth-century architecture in *The Architectural Heritage of Newport, Rhode Island*, Antoinette Downing and Vincent Scully noted: "The tastes of a wealthy seafaring merchant society stamped these new buildings with a provincial and matter of fact, almost burgher lavishness. Newport building, like Newport furniture, now developed a quality of intrinsic richness wherein ornament became an inseparable part of the whole."

"Burgher lavishness" is an apt description for the showplace Metcalf Bowler built for himself on Clark Street in 1758. A Georgian town house of grand proportions, it has a boldly ornamented facade. That facades were of concern to Metcalf Bowler is apparent from both his vocations—his known profession as a successful merchant and his clandestine occupation as a British double agent moving freely in Newport's open, new-money society. Whichever guise he wore, his house assured that in the eyes of the world Metcalf Bowler would be seen as a man of style and taste.

The house's bold exterior embellishment is so dominant that the overall fine symmetry and proportions of the house may not at first register. The attic dormers catch the eye first. Crowned by robust

A dramatic shaft of morning sunlight reveals examples of eighteenth-century carving artistry, wrought by an unknown craftsman: the volutes and raised panels of the hallway arch and the sculptural dentil cornice above. The fixture on the wall is a Venetian reflecting sconce.

129

semicircular-headed windows, the dormers give the roofline an assertive presence that is underscored by the carved cornice below. More decorative than the cornices found on many colonial Georgian houses, this carved work combines emphatic modillions with pearl-like dentils. Under the cornice, the entire exterior surface of the house is alive with the crisscross groovings of wood finished to look like stonework. In 1758 this rusticated wall surface would have been the very latest architectural fashion to be imported from England. A man concerned with appearances, Metcalf Bowler must have relished showing off the costly, skillfully executed faux stone exterior to Newport's merchant society.

Inside, the house reveals highly refined structural detailing. A regally wide center hall leads to a fine carved staircase lit by an arched Palladian-inspired window. The front parlors at each side of the center hall also boast elegantly carved wainscots, moldings, and detailing.

In one parlor, frescoed eighteenth-century chinoiserie panels ornament the walls. The quality of these panels, and their survival, is one of the features that makes this house notable to American decorative arts experts today. As a result of trade with the Orient, a vogue for oriental lacquer-work screens, furniture, and accessories spread throughout Europe and America in the eighteenth century. Eventually, American and European artisans perfected their own versions of this ornamental work; consequently the panels in this house may be Western examples. Dating from the 1720s, the panels are in a section of the house that predates the 1758 construction. As often happened in the colonial period, Metcalf Bowler built his house on a seventeenth-century foundation and partial structure, which must have contained the frescoed panels.

When Metcalf Bowler died in the 1770s, his house was sold to William Vernon, another prosperous merchant. During Vernon's ownership the house came into the political limelight. In 1780 it became the headquarters of General Jean Baptiste de Rochambeau, the commander of the French forces who fought with the colonists during the Revolution. Both George Washington and the Marquis de Lafayette, a volunteer in the Continental army, were frequent visitors to the house. It was here that they first conceived the idea for the battle of Yorktown, Virginia, which forced the surrender of the British general, Cornwallis.

When he built the house in the eighteenth century, Metcalf Bowler reserved most of the architectural showmanship for the parts of the house that others would see. The rich sculptural wall carving in this parlor, which faces the street, would have been appreciated by both visitors and passersby. Now a sitting room, its continental flavor is imparted by the French sofa and chairs and the Italian and Flemish paintings. The side chairs against the wall were made in Ireland in the 1800s in the Chippendale style of the 1700s.

With its handsome arched molding, the built-in corner cupboard in the dining room (LEFT) is characteristic of a design that became popular with the advent of Georgian architecture in the 1700s. Around the satin-wood table is a set of reproduction Italian Empire chairs with gracefully curved backs. The 1750s Philadelphia highboy came down through the owner's family.

An Oriental runner provides a jewel-like pattern on the floor of the upstairs hall, where a rush-seated chair, Empire country table, and deacon's bench—all nineteenth-century pieces—are arranged in an eye-pleasing grouping (RIGHT).

In the same way that he made sure that the more frequently seen downstairs front rooms received architectural embellishment, Metcalf Bowler saw to it that the second floor bedrooms at the front of the house were well ornamented. Not only is the chimney breast decorated with elegantly restrained carving, but the fireplace is tiled with handpainted ceramic Dutch tiles. The bed and washstand in the master bedroom (RIGHT) are part of a Victorian set that the owner's great uncle used in his room at college.

William Vernon's family continued to own the house until the late-nineteenth century. At the turn of the century the house was taken over by a charitable institution, which owned it until 1964, when it was purchased by Margaretta and Quinto Maganini.

Consulting with Antoinette Downing, an authority on Newport architecture, Margaretta Maganini returned the house to the way it looked in the late-eighteenth century. Exterior shutters that had been incorrectly added to all the windows and front door in the nineteenth century were removed, and the house was listed on the National Register for Historic Places. In 1982, the Maganinis' daughter, Margaretta Clulow, became the present owner of the house.

Margaretta Clulow has made Vernon House a comfortable home for her family without sacrificing her fondest wish: to furnish and decorate the house as it might have appeared in the eighteenth century. The guidelines she has set for the project include antiques, but they must be sturdy and usable. European and Oriental furniture and objects are on her wish list in order to reflect the urbane international character of a colonial Newport merchant's house.

Maintaining the house keeps her occupied with twentieth-century realities, however. The recent discovery that both chimneys were crumbling necessitated extensive repair work. The outside of the house also needed repainting. Replicating the original stone-gray color required mixing a blend of paint and black sand, thereby duplicating the sandy concoction used in the eighteenth century when merchant ships carried black volcanic sand from the South Seas as ballast. Sometime after the house was painted, Margaretta Clulow realized the painter had done an expert job when she heard someone on the street outside tapping the wall to see if it was really stone. It would have pleased Metcalf Bowler to know that yet another person had been fooled by his facade.

A paving of blue and white delft tiles (LEFT) enriches the fireplace of the master bedroom. Prized in the eighteenth century as they are today, these hand-decorated tiles are another sign of the prosperity of the builder of Vernon House.

An arched Palladian-inspired window at the back of the house provides abundant daylight to show the way up the stairs leading to the second floor. The ends of each stair are ornamented with a carved scroll. The use of three different types of spiral turnings in the balusters was fashionable in New England houses until nearly the end of the eighteenth century. Such balusters were often carved by sailors at sea and sold ashore for extra money.

The wainscoted dado along the wall opposite the stair rail is a feature found in fine stairways of New England Georgian houses. This dado has particularly fine shallow relief carving, executed as a series of short pilasters joined by horizontal rail-like bands.

Isaac Peck House

AN 1809 TWO-FAMILY HOUSE RECONFIGURED IN PROVIDENCE

I
t was a rather modest dwelling in its day, an unassuming two-flat tenement built for working-class families. The builder was Isaac Peck, an apparently industrious teamster who hauled loads along the bustling Providence waterfront from the 1790s to the early 1800s. An anonymous little house of understated Federal lines, the construction was nevertheless sound and sure. It was Isaac Peck's third known building effort. The first house he built in Providence was a large two-family house that still stands today on Wickenden Street, in the city's Fox Point section. Located a few blocks to the north, this third, more compact two-family house was constructed shortly after Isaac Peck purchased the land in 1809. Most probably the teamster built the dwelling for his son, George, whose family owned the house for more than seventy-five years. Unfortunately, no records survive to indicate who might have shared the house with George Peck's family.

One of the oldest sections of Providence, Fox Point was part of the original colonial settlement established in 1636 shortly after Roger Williams arrived from the Massachusetts Bay Colony. Although farming was an economic mainstay of most of Rhode Island throughout the seventeenth and eighteenth centuries, the economy of Providence naturally looked to the waterfront. At first, Providence played second fiddle to Newport, with her commerce growing on a small scale. Providence merchants were enterprising, however, and they began to bring in goods from Boston and New York, as well as

The modest 1809 Isaac Peck House (LEFT), originally was built as a two-family dwelling. A side-hall internal plan dictated an off-center doorway, yet windows and door have nevertheless been designed in a harmoniously symmetrical exterior arrangement.

The aesthetic appeal of many New England house facades lies in what is eliminated. The sole decoration on this facade is the restrained pure geometry of the Doric style pilasters and short pillars on each side of the front door (RIGHT).

The owners refinished the original 1809 banister on which even the newel post was intact (ABOVE). The artisan who restored the house was able to re-create the nineteenth-century wainscoting of the stairwall by detecting its shape under the old plaster. In this modest house, none of the wainscoting was ever panelled.

A blazing fire casts its cheerful glow over the living room (TOP RIGHT). Above the Pembroke table by the fireplace is a framed silk embroidery. The Seth Thomas pillar and scroll clock on the mantel was crafted in the nineteenth century.

The daintily ornamented Sheraton style mirror in the living room is a centennial piece, made in the late-nineteenth century, the same vintage as the Martha Washington chair beside it (BOTTOM RIGHT).

from Newport to trade in the large countryside around Providence. By the end of the 1700s, Providence overtook Newport and, as the new century approached, readied herself for the significant role she would play in New England's industrial growth.

As an expanding commercial center, Providence attracted a large middle class of diverse backgrounds. Thus, throughout the nineteenth century Fox Point had a growing population of Irish, Portuguese, and Cape Verdian immigrants who worked as laborers on the docks or in the factories that began to be built in the early 1800s. Many of these working people lived in rental properties like the two-family houses Isaac Peck built. As often happens in tenement districts, many of the houses were changed and reworked throughout the late-nineteenth and early-twentieth centuries, eventually falling into neglect and dilapidation.

But even in the 1950s the College Hill section of Fox Point, where Isaac Peck's 1809 house is located, had begun to turn around. That was when the area was designated as an historic district. Then, in the late 1970s and early 1980s, College Hill became the focus of a concerted preservation effort. One by one, the old houses were rescued and rehabilitated. Old woodwork was re-created; original paint colors were duplicated. Today, the refurbishment of these old working-class houses has turned College Hill into a showcase urban neighborhood.

Isaac Peck's house is a shining example of College Hill's restorations. The work was undertaken by the present owners, who began the year-long endeavor shortly after purchasing the house in 1981.

In the dining room (ABOVE), the original mantel and all the woodwork was painted a gray-green color that exactly duplicates the color the room was painted in 1809. The original color was discovered by scraping through several layers of old paint. The furniture in the dining room includes nineteenth-century European chairs, and a handsome Sheraton chest. A collection of English ceramics in the shape of early American houses is lined up along the mantelpiece.

Glistening nineteenth-century American silver tea balls, strainers, and cups are arranged in a cupboard in the dining room (RIGHT).

While not wanting to re-create a two-family house, they were intent on restoring lost and decayed structural elements and recapturing the original architectural character of the 1809 structure.

The house is organized in a side-hall plan, one especially well suited to the double house, a new type of dwelling that became popular in the early-nineteenth century. Most double houses, however, were designed in a two-story, side-by-side scheme, the side halls of each dwelling sharing a common wall. This house, however, had one flat on the first floor, and the other, above, with the two sharing a common entry. Although the first and second floors are no longer separate units, the restoration brought back enough of the original structural plan so that the entry is today exactly the same as it was in the 1800s. When the doors to the living room and kitchen are closed, one can see how the entry functioned as a common area for two tenant families.

Because this is now a one-family house, room designations have

The mellow wood of a country Pennsylvania cupboard and wideboard chestnut table gives the kitchen an inviting feeling. The painted New England chairs around the table date from about 1800.

Now a welcoming feature of the kitchen, the original fireplace (LEFT) was uncovered in the recent restoration of the house. Although the original brick and stonework survived years of concealment, the nineteenth-century mantel had to be re-created. An exact reproduction was made by following the design of one in a neighboring house. The copper kettle and pots arranged around the fireplace are mostly New England-crafted utensils. The nineteenth-century Salem rocker still displays its original painted decoration.

Outlined in the rose-gold light of a fire in the bedroom hearth are the railings and posts of an 1840 cannonball style bed. A Pennsylvania blanket box sits on the floor in front of the bed.

been changed from their original 1809 uses. The dining room, which opens to the left of the entry, was originally a parlor, and what is now the living room is made up of an original bedroom and a second bedroom that had been added in 1900.

The owners also altered the layout of the original kitchen to make more efficient use of space. In 1809, a small bedroom and a pantry area were situated off the kitchen. Both spaces were combined with the main kitchen in the recent restoration. The original kitchen fireplace was a lucky discovery. Boarded up an unknown number of years ago, it still had all the original brickwork and stone hearth intact.

Since it was in very run-down condition when the owners bought it, the house required extensive structural repair. The roof was leaking badly and floors were crumbling. Fortunately, the owners secured the expertise of a local artisan who had restored other College Hill houses. He set up a workshop in the dining room and worked steadily for almost a year on the project. Through the years, most of the original woodwork, including doors and windows, were replaced with twentieth-century elements, and one of the artisan's main tasks was to create substitutes crafted in an accurate nineteenth-century design. He made the replications by studying existing architectural features in similar period houses on College Hill, as well as by removing layers of old paint in the Isaac Peck House to see the outlines of the original woodwork.

Compared to the restoration, furnishing the house was easy. The owners simply filled the rooms with the English and American nineteenth-century antiques they had been collecting for years. The patina of their antique furniture and the luster of their groupings of china and silver bring a friendly charm to the pristinely restored rooms of the little Federal house.

Dedicated preservationists, the owners confess that this is only the most recent of several old house renovations they have undertaken. Each one has offered rewards far beyond the satisfaction of restoring doors and floors and banishing neglect. The real gratification lies in ensuring the continuity of an antique house's own individual legacy. In the restored Isaac Peck House, a working man's dwelling has reasserted its unpretentious and very Yankee character.

MAINE

Norsemen sailing along the New England seaboard in AD 1000 were possibly the first Europeans to note Maine's rugged, irregular coastline. Pinnacles of pre-glacial mountains near the shore form 2,000 islands. The name "Maine" came about as "main land" to distinguish it from these offshore islands, as well as being a compliment to Queen Henrietta Maria, Charles I's wife, who owned the province of Mayne in France. Neal R. Peirce and Jerry Hagstrom have written in The Book of America: "As the crow flies, the distance between Kittery, on the New Hampshire border, to Eastport, beside New Brunswick, is only two hundred and twenty-eight miles. But if one were to follow each bay and cove and inlet, one would see a shoreline of more than three thousand, five hundred miles."

The coast of this, the largest of the New England states, is romantic, beautiful, and much painted. The hinterlands of Maine are mountainous, thickly forested, and remote.

It is believed that the Italian navigator and explorer Giovanni Caboto (1450–1498), who, after settling in England and anglicizing his name to John Cabot, cruised along the North American coast, thinking it to be part of Asia. The first authenticated explorer was Giovanni da Verrazano (1485?–1528?) of Florence, who passed Maine on his exploration of Narragansett Bay and New York. He was followed by others who were lured by tales of a legendary and wealthy city called Norumbega, supposedly on the Penebscot River. The first English settlers arrived in 1607 and built a settlement at the mouth of the Kennebec River, which they named St. George's Fort. While there, the settlers built the first English ship to be constructed in North America, a thirty-ton pinnace they christened the *Virginia*, but diseases and the fierce cold of Maine forced the few survivors to abandon the colony after a year.

The first permanent colony to be established by the English was Pemaquid on Muscongus Bay. However, the colony of Massachusetts annexed most of Maine during the seventeenth century. The seat of government was therefore remote, as were troops to guard against the constant threat of Indian attack. The French and Indian Wars ravaged Maine's early settlements. A century later when the Revolutionary War took place, Maine was to suffer again. However, from the Massachusetts government, Maine early gained a public school system, though this was countered by harsh religious laws, virulent anti-Roman Catholicism, and hidebound conventional morality.

The inhabitants of Maine developed a wary attitude unlike the conviviality associated with most Americans. Their isolation forced a spirit of rugged independence. Luxury of the kind seen in Boston or Newport did not exist in Portsmouth, Maine's major seaport, until late in the eighteenth century, when Maine began to prosper from the seafaring trades and the colony's meager population burgeoned.

During the seventeenth and first half of the eighteenth centuries, most of the inhabitants of Maine lived in simple houses. A type of house that was found in Maine as well as in other parts of New England was the garrison house. According to Allen G. Noble in *Wood, Brick & Stone*, this was first named by historical investigators who assumed that these houses were built for defense because of their second story overhang, a feature found in forts and blockhouses. However, as there are no openings that would have allowed for defensive action, and the overhang usually appears only on one or, at most, two sides, the name is deceptive. The overhang would appear to be based on European medieval house forms; the overhang offered protection from wind-driven rain for only the streetside walls of half-timbered houses and also gave greater floor area on the second story, an advantage in crowded European town houses. As garrison houses in New England were weatherboarded, not half-timbered, and space was easily come by, the rationale for the garrison house form was outmoded. The floor plan consisted of two equal-sized rooms divided by a central chimney and a small entrance hall. One room on the ground floor would be used as a kitchen and family room, the other as a bedroom and more public, formal room. The second floor would be divided into two bedrooms.

Evolving also in New England, and represented in this section by the Thomas Perkins House on the Kennebunk River, is the saltbox house, named because its sloping roof was similar to the lids of the wooden boxes that contained blocks of salt. (In the South, similarly formed roofs are called catslides.) The earliest of these houses came about because a lean-to shed was added to the kitchen side of the house and the roof line was extended down over this addition. Later houses were designed from the start to have this extra back room and the sloping roof made all of a piece. These houses had the typical early colonial central chimney, and generally had five rooms on the ground floor but a very small amount of headroom on the second floor because of the sloping roof.

Because of its remoteness, Maine's houses remained humble and less affected by fashionable architectural styles longer than houses in Massachusetts, Connecticut, or Rhode Island. However, by the second half of the eighteenth century, when destruction from the French and Indian Wars had passed and growing affluence from the seafaring trade had begun, seaports like Portsmouth had developed a pool of shipwrights and housewrights, blacksmiths, masons, mechanics, and artisans. To accommodate larger families, the well-to-do in Maine began to build larger houses which were directly inspired by the Georgian architecture in England that had spread to America via style books. These houses had varied plans according to the wealth of the builder and the number of rooms required, but they all show a classical symmetry, typical of Georgian style. The chimney remained central in the earliest forms, the front door was central, and the windows were balanced in equal number on either side. Windows on the second floor duplicated those on the ground floor. Such a house is Farnsworth in Waldoboro, Maine, built in 1760.

All these Maine houses were built of wood from the colony's all-enveloping forests. White pine, oak, cedar, poplar, hemlock, and many other species covered the mountains. These woods were also used to make furniture, for the inhabitants of Maine were less likely to import fancy English pieces than their colonists to the south. Maine produced its own cabinetmakers, such as Samuel Winthrop Benjamin, born in 1786. But Maine always remained unique, isolated, and less sophisticated than its neighbors in its style and its artifacts. Not surprisingly,

furniture of a folk-art type emerged from Maine toward the end of the nineteenth century, carved in a simple, geometric style not far from tramp art and painted in fantasy wood graining. Original to the state, this furniture is much collected today.

In James A. Michener's book *U.S.A.* there is a quotation from *The Salt Book*, written by Kennebunkport teenagers in 1973: "The people of Kennebunkport have always done for themselves. In the past, they've built their own boats, raised their own food and preserved it, chopped the wood for their stoves, tapped their trees for maple syrup, and made the snowshoes they needed to reach the sugarbush in February." This dogged independence, shaped by the geography and the history of the state of Maine is reflected in the houses of the colonists.

Thomas Perkins House

A 1724 SALTBOX ON THE BANKS OF THE KENNEBUNK RIVER

At the time Thomas Perkins built this house on the banks of the Kennebunk River, the hardships confronting new settlers to the region were formidable indeed. The land was still very much a wilderness—the nearest settlement, the town of Arundel, was ten miles away—and the threat posed by the Indians who claimed the land as their birthright was considerable.

One can only speculate as to Thomas Perkins's reasons for selecting so remote a location for his house; he left behind no journals or letters that offer any explanation. According to town records, however, around 1724 the land on which the house was built was owned by his father, another Thomas Perkins, who had settled in Arundel in 1720. It is reasonable to conclude, therefore, that the younger Thomas—a bit more venturesome than his father—simply chose to strike out on an unchartered course of sorts, though he most likely did so in the hopes that he would soon be joined by other settlers.

Cape Porpus was the name of the area in the early 1600s. It is said that porpoises were seen by the English fishermen who came across the north Atlantic, attracted by the rich catches to be found in the waters off Maine's coast. What began as a temporary fishermen's coastal outpost, gradually grew into a settlement in the mid-seventeenth century. But like many other settlements throughout New England it was abandoned during the Indian wars of the late 1600s. The settlers who returned to the area in the early-eighteenth century

The stately, central-chimney house built by Thomas Perkins in 1724 sits high on a knoll above the Kennebunk River (LEFT). The front entrance and single windows are original; the enclosed porch to the left was added in the 1960s. In the foreground is a Concord grape arbor.

To one side of the house is an old shingled barn, used primarily for storage (RIGHT).

moved inland to establish farms along the Kennebunk River and re-named the settlement Arundel.

That name, according to legend, was chosen as a gesture to an Englishman, the Earl of Arundel. The young earl, it seems, had mar-ried a woman deemed unsuitable by his family. His wife, pregnant with the couple's first child, retreated to the home of relatives at Cape Porpus. Both she and the baby died in childbirth, but to express his appreciation for the kindness shown his wife, the earl gave the town a bell—a vital means of communication in colonial settlements. In grat-itude the townspeople renamed their settlement Arundel after the earl. More than a hundred years later in 1821, the town was again rechristened, this time as Kennebunkport, a name derived from a local Indian term meaning "long cut bank."

Among those who resettled Arundel in the early 1700s was Thomas Perkins's father, who had come from Greenland, New Hamp-shire, to renew a land grant his own father was given in 1687. In addition to the land he secured through the grant renewal, the elder Thomas Perkins acquired a sizable parcel from the heirs of William Reynolds and from others who had first settled the town. The Rey-nolds heirs, however, had also sold a portion of this land to Stephen Hardy, a blacksmith by trade, and Perkins and Hardy became em-broiled in a prolonged dispute over its ownership. Though title was awarded to Thomas Perkins in the end, the two men long harbored ill feelings. They buried their animosity, however, when Perkins's son, Thomas, married Hardy's daughter, Lydia.

The young couple moved to the property on the banks of the

The clapboard saltbox is distinguished by a simple silhouette and sturdy wood construction (ABOVE).

Situated within easy proximity to the drive-way, the side door entry (RIGHT) is not original to the house. It is, how-ever, at least a hundred years old, for it appears in photographs taken of the house during the nine-teenth century.

158

A pump draws water from one of three wells on the property. Surprisingly close to the briny river's edge, the well provides fresh water for a nearby patch of raspberries.

The Perkins family cemetery (RIGHT) is nestled beneath the trees just a few yards from the banks of the river. Thomas and Lydia Perkins are buried here, as are their children and a number of their grandchildren.

A copper weather vane tops the roof of the barn (FAR RIGHT).

The side entry (LEFT), which opens into a narrow hallway, is used as the primary entrance today. The inlayed Hepplewhite desk dates from the nineteenth century. The Dutch door leads to the kitchen.

The glass-enclosed porch at the rear of the house was added during the 1960s to open interiors to panoramic views of the Kennebunk River. Meals are often taken here, and it is a good spot for bird watching (TOP RIGHT).

One of the original rooms of the house is the living room (BOTTOM RIGHT), which has doors leading to the kitchen and to a small study. The ladder-back chairs and tea table are family antiques that work well with the elegant furnishings of the rest of the room. The couch is covered with English chintz and the lamps are painted English tin-ware.

Kennebunk where Thomas Perkins, Sr., had already built a house in the 1720s. Around 1724 they built their own saltbox-shaped farmhouse on the river from land the senior Perkins would deed to his son in 1727. By granting the young Thomas Perkins a parcel of fifty acres, the elder Perkins enabled his son to become a proprietor of Arundel. Proprietors were those who possessed at least fifty acres of land, a circumstance that conferred power and status in colonial New England. As one of the largest landowners in the community, Thomas Perkins would have had decision-making power in municipal affairs, as the elected selectmen do in New England towns today. In colonial times, landownership—not the popular vote—was what determined who held power.

Thomas and Lydia Perkins developed their property into one of Arundel's finest farmsteads. The surrounding area developed rather slowly, but eventually a river village did develop, its growth hastened in part by the establishment of the mill built by two of Thomas and

Typical of early colonial houses built with a central chimney, the front door opens into a small hall and enclosed staircase. The door to the right leads to the dining room.

The dining room's built-in corner cabinets and encased beam are evidence of the modifications made during the Victorian era. The Hitchcock chairs and side tables were inherited from the owners' families. The ancestral portraits were executed by eighteenth-century portraitist Alvin Jasper Conant. The large circular dining table is on loan from a friend who convinced the owners it was precisely the table the room required.

The kitchen, which was probably used as a storage space of some type during Thomas Perkins's day, is a welcoming space where friends and family often gather. A tin chandelier hangs over the thick pine trestle table and slat-back chairs. The brick wall—once hidden beneath wood panelling—has been uncovered by the present owners, who also added the woodburning stove. The cupboard doors were fashioned from the remnants of the panelling.

Lydia's sons. By the mid-nineteenth century, Kennebunkport would become an important shipbuilding center, and commerce would progress briskly along the Kennebunk River.

Thomas died in 1752 at the age of fifty-two. His son James was the next to gain ownership of the house; he served as an officer in the Revolutionary War but by 1787 had become a merchant sea captain. James died in 1825 at the age of eighty-two, leaving the house to his son Tristram. Tristram never married, however, and upon his death in 1880 at the age of seventy-nine, the house became the property of his nephew, Henry Perkins. Two years later, Henry sold the house to a William Peabody, the first nonfamily member to acquire it in more than 175 years.

Today, the property has the appearance of a small riverfront estate; the land has not been farmed for several decades and the fields have given way to stretches of lawn. But the farmhouse—a simple, handsome, sound structure—remains substantially true to Thomas Perkins's plan. This plan conformed to the central-chimney arrangement that was so common to New England's colonial houses. Thomas Perkins's objective, quite understandably, was to erect a simple, sturdy structure that would adequately shelter his family for many years to come. Its design resembled numerous houses being built throughout the New England colonies. The front door opened into a small hall and enclosed staircase; the keeping room was to the right, the parlor, to the left, and the bedrooms, above. The chimney was situated in the middle of the house and the fireplaces for all of the rooms were built into this chimney.

The house was enlarged at some point—presumably by Thomas Perkins—with the saltbox addition and also bears evidence of minor modifications made during the Victorian era. A glass-enclosed porch was added to the rear of the house in the 1960s, but, having been deftly incorporated into the saltbox design, complements the colonial architecture.

The present owners purchased the house in 1980, moving there from a large house in Kennebunkport where they raised their children. They wanted a smaller house in the same area and were attracted to the old farmhouse and its riverside setting. The work the

A bedroom occupies part of the space that served as the original sleeping quarters. The fireplace in this room has been altered through the years; it was originally twice as large. The antique furnishings comprise a mix of family heirlooms and pieces acquired through the years. The spool bed is covered with a nineteenth-century Wisconsin quilt. The inlaid desk is a Hepplewhite.

A daybed tucked beneath an attic skylight (ABOVE), added during the 1960s, is an ideal spot for curling up with a good book or simply watching the clouds drift by. The nineteenth-century quilt is from Elmira, New York; the pillows were handmade by the owner.

The attic was converted into quarters for the owners' college-age sons. This attic bath, a Victorian renovation to the house, is decorated in Victorian spirit (BELOW).

house demanded of them has been largely cosmetic, and the grounds, which include the Perkins family cemetery, have been altered only by the addition of an apple orchard.

Much as Thomas and Lydia Perkins most probably furnished the house—with simple, comfortable pieces—so, too, have these owners. Their furnishings, many of them antiques, are comprised of both family heirlooms and pieces acquired at auctions. The interior design is uncontrived and unaffected—a scheme well suited to this simple colonial structure. Rather than trying to recapture the ambience of a particular period, the owners have chosen simply to mix the various pieces they've assembled through the years in an agreeable blend.

The structural modifications made by previous occupants will remain. The present owners feel a strong commitment to preserving the house as it has evolved, and believe that any evidence of change enhances the structural character of the house. "Although we are certainly conscious of the past, we think of the house in terms of its present and future," says one of the owners. "It has never been a desire of ours to restore it to what it was in Thomas Perkins's day. There is no point to that. The fact that the house has continued intact through the years is to Thomas Perkins's credit. And he would probably be the first to agree that any house, if it is to survive, must adapt to the demands of the time."

169

Farnsworth

A 1760 CENTER-CHIMNEY HOUSE IN WALDOBORO

I t is called Farnsworth, a name born of recent times, but one quite fitting for the south coast farm once claimed by three generations that bore that name. The first of these Farnsworths—a patriot, pioneer, and gentleman—was originally from Groton, Massachusetts. William Farnsworth first saw the hundred-acre tract while serving as an Indian scout in the 1750s at Fort St. Georges in Thomaston. The territory then known as Broad Bay was first settled by the Germans in the 1740s, but the settlement had disintegrated as a consequence of attacks during the French and Indian War. It was not until the mid-1750s that a small group of settlers returned to reestablish their homesteads. However, because the warring factions continued to threaten settlement, scouts from the wilderness fort ten miles away made their way to Broad Bay to guard the settlers during the daylight hours while they cleared their land and planted or harvested their crops. William Farnsworth was among the scouts who helped to protect the Broad Bay settlement, and it was while he was engaged in this effort that he discovered the coastal stretch that he was determined to make his own. In 1760 William Farnsworth bought the land from Samuel Waldo and set about establishing his farm.

During the same year, he married Elizabeth Rutherford, daughter of the Presbyterian minister at the fort, and they broke ground for the farmhouse that still stands today. Elizabeth Farnsworth bore him three sons, William, Isaac, and Robert, all three of whom were given

This side entrance to the house (LEFT) is now used regularly. The section to the left of the door is the original structure; the portion into which the door opens is of more recent vintage, added during the 1930s.

The house that William Farnsworth built in 1760 is a classic two-story, central-chimney Georgian farmhouse that looks out on the expanse of Maine's Broad Bay (RIGHT). The first clapboard house to be built in the area, it features a wood "cord" ornament around the double-hipped roof and twelve-over-eight windows.

shares of their father's land and took pride, as did he, in farming it. In 1780 the eldest, William, wed Abigail Fairfield Stuart, a widow four years his senior who had two daughters of her own and bore seven more children after marrying William—six daughters and a son, also named William.

The second William Farnsworth had great hopes that his son would follow in his footsteps and prosper in farming, but like many of his generation, William Farnsworth III was drawn to the sea and was resolved to make his fortune as a sea captain. As a consequence of this resolve, and his eventual death at sea in 1826, his share of the farm was sold for one hundred and fifty dollars to pay his debts. More than a century would pass before the hundred acres his grandfather had first claimed would be returned to its original configuration by a single owner.

It is the present owner, Mary Louise Meyer, who named the farm Farnsworth when she and her late husband purchased the farm in 1962. Mary Louise Meyer is an amateur historian and is a member of the Farnsworth Museum in Rockland, which is named for the fourth William Farnsworth born on the farm. The Meyers were taken by the property's rich past and bought the property as a country retreat and escape. The house came completely furnished right down to the silverware, and they were dedicated to maintaining it as it was.

The Georgian style house is the same farmhouse Colonel Farnsworth built in 1760, updated certainly, but still very much as he designed it. It was one of the first clapboard houses built in the area after the destructive French and Indian Wars. The early-eighteenth

From this approach to the house (ABOVE) one sees Farnsworth's barn—the original structure except for the roof and door. The old original barn was on the verge of collapsing when the Meyers acquired the property, and new foundations and supporting beams were replaced.

There are numerous apple trees, most of them varieties no longer found commercially, on Farnsworth's grounds, and the apples are often gathered for baking (RIGHT).

Because the front entry is no longer used as the main entrance, the front step, a very old millstone, has assumed the role of garden sculpture, its cracks and apertures welcoming wildflowers. A wooden decoy sits inside the open door.

The parlor (LEFT) is decorated in a relaxed country manner to encourage all who step into the room to make themselves completely at home. The upholstered pieces in the room are slipcovered in a foam green chintz that is compatible with the vibrant blues in the adjoining dining room. The floor is protected by braided rugs and one old hooked rug. The country side table, graced with antique books and flowers, was made of New England pine in the 1800s. A framed antique map of Maine hangs above the table.

The simplicity of the structural detailing is underscored by the white walls in the parlor (ABOVE); furniture such as the maple rocker, pine table, and spinning wheel complement the room perfectly.

The dining room, or ships' room, as the family calls it, was painted this nautical shade of blue when they first saw the house, and it is a color they have chosen to maintain (LEFT and RIGHT). The one change the owners made in the dining room was to the floor, which they painted a deep blue—"the color of the sea," says Mary Louise Meyer. Hardly typical of floors found in New England colonial houses, it seems, however, the perfect counterpoint to the walls.

Spaces in the Farnsworth house are carefully used, as evidenced by the plate racks built into the small passage between the dining room and pantry that display an impressive collection of blue and white platters (RIGHT).

The pantry's shelves hold a wonderful miscellany of china and glassware, an abundance of which is patterned in traditional blue and white motifs (FAR RIGHT).

An unexpected shade of blue also appears in an upstairs guest room, which is painted a robin's egg hue. The pine furnishings are of nineteenth-century vintage and are thought to have been crafted by New England furniture makers.

century had witnessed the arrival in the colonies of the Georgian style, an elegant design influence that developed in England during the reign of the four Hanoverian kings—George I, George II, George III, and George IV—who ruled successively from 1714 to 1830. A sophisticated approach distinguished by graceful lines and proportions, the Georgian style exhibited a refinement of detailing that was hitherto lacking in American homes. Carved moldings, panelled doors and wainscoting, and elaborately carved mantels began to appear more frequently, though houses in rural communities retained a greater simplicity than their urban counterparts.

Organized in a center-hall plan, the original section of house includes the living room, dining room, kitchen and scullery, and

borning room. A guest bedroom and bath on the first floor, and three bedrooms and a bath upstairs were added in the 1950s. Originally the second floor consisted of two front bedrooms and a large, open sleeping loft with a separate, enclosed bedroom at one end that was reserved for the eldest daughter in the house. It was customary in colonial times for the oldest daughter to be given a room of her own, a custom that no doubt generated no small amount of envy among William Farnsworth's remaining six children.

Because the Meyers appreciated the antiques they inherited with their purchase, they kept the room schemes unchanged. Instead, after adding an antique or two of their own, they concentrated on caring for the land—a considerable tract indeed—and on adding to

Antique doorstops such as
this one are found in
nearly every room—a
necessity in an old house
with sloping floors and
doors that have begun to
lean a bit in their frames.

179

With its deep red hues and mellowed woods and faded fabrics, the living room (ABOVE) is where the family relaxes together, especially in the light of an autumn evening's fire. This room was once the original kitchen. The new kitchen was added in the 1930s. The fireplace is original, although it has undergone restorative work in years past. The desk added by the Meyers, is eighteenth-century cherry; the hooked rugs were made by New England craftsmen.

or improving upon the other buildings on the property. The barn, for example, was rebuilt; the foundations says Mary Louise Meyer, were rotting away, but the main structure was saved and "patched," using as much old wood as could be found. The Meyers also built a small guest house/studio near the edge of the property on Farnsworth Point and moved a small building purchased in a neighboring town onto the property for use as a library. This building is a rustic little structure that is a favorite retreat of the Meyers' grandchildren, and though it is filled with books, it has the ambience more of a treehouse or cabin than of a library of any sort.

Now Mary Louise Meyer is concentrating on researching details of the Farnsworth's lives so that she can at last piece together a complete history of the place she calls Farnsworth. "There is very little written of the Farnsworths, and I feel that this—a written history—is one part of the legacy that I can contribute," she says. "I'd like to think that when my grandchildren are grown, they can stand here and have a strong, clear sense of what this land meant to William Farnsworth and his descendants and appreciate what it will be to future generations."

The house enjoys splendid views of the bay that brought William Farnsworth to this place (ABOVE).

The bay window of the living room is not an original structural element, but it does open the room to views of the gardens and woods. The small chest in the corner is a sea captain's desk (LEFT).

181

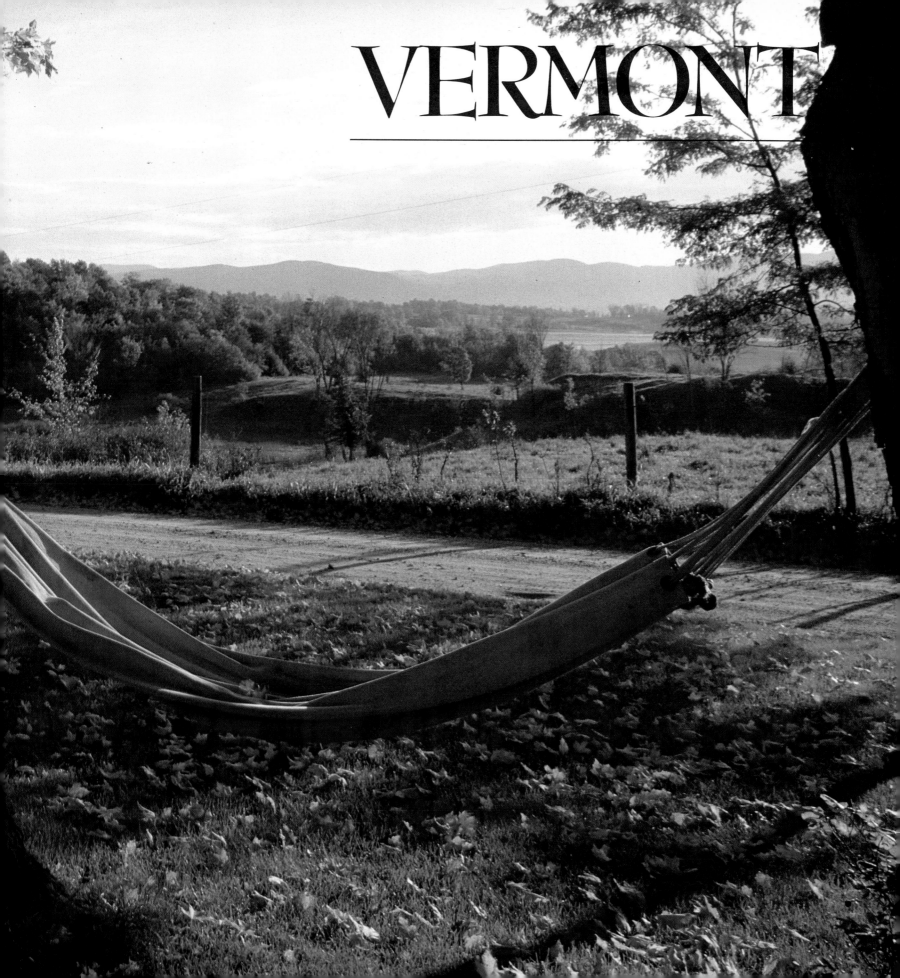

VERMONT

Nowadays many people think of Vermont as a resort area. Its rigorous but bracing climate, its pure air and clear streams lure visitors all year round. Heavy snowfalls in winter produce great skiing conditions, and the mountains and lakes are perfect for hiking and swimming in the summer. The small, picturesque farmhouses dotted about the landscape give a folk-art impression. Even the woodpiles in Vermont seem more neatly stacked than in any other New England state.

Tucked up against the Canadian border of French-speaking Quebec, the area was up for grabs in the early days of colonial settlement. In 1609 French explorer Samuel de Champlain journeyed to Vermont and named Lake Champlain in the northwestern corner of the territory. In 1655 the French established a fort on Isle la Motte in Lake Champlain and used this as a base to fight the antagonistic Iroquois. Fort Drummer, an English settlement, was established in the southeastern corner of Vermont by the Massachusetts Bay Colony, near to present-day Brattleboro, and four years later, a trading post was opened there. The tug of war for Vermont lasted through the French and Indian Wars. Though the French had abandoned all their posts in Vermont by 1758, they left the legacy of Vermont's name, "Vert Mont," or green mountain.

From the beginning of the eighteenth century New Hampshire and New York had quarreled over the ownership of the Vermont region. According to Oscar Theodore Barck, Jr. and Hugh Talmage Lefler in *Colonial America*, England, still in control, decided in favor of the New York claim, but New Hampshire refused to accept the verdict. At the outbreak of the Revolution, patriot Ethan Allen and his volunteer militia called the Green Mountain Boys—originally organized to fight New York's claim to the region—surprised and captured Fort Ticonderoga in New York state. Allen forced the surrender of the British commander. The Vermonters hoped this action would be rewarded with statehood. The Continental Congress was so divided on the issue of statehood for Vermont that, when peace came, Ethan Allen re-

opened talks with the English. There is speculation as to whether he did this to force Congress to come to a decision, or whether he believed that through the English he could obtain independent statehood plus lucrative trading with Canada, his neighbor to the north. For this negotiation he was charged with treason, which was never proved. As Barck and Lefler admit, "There is a growing belief that if Vermont had received all the concessions from England that she desired, she would not have become the fourteenth state."

Being New England's only inland state, Vermont was dependent for transport on either the Connecticut River to the east, or the majestic Lake Champlain to the west. The earliest settlements, such as the 1680 saltbox house in Windsor County, or the 1792 Elijah Wright farmhouse near Lake Champlain, tended to be close to these waterways. As in the rest of New England, the earliest permanent structures in Vermont were simple one- or two-room farmhouses, medieval in style, with a central chimney and a huge, smoky fireplace. These early houses had steeply pitched roofs, a style originating in England, where the roofs were made of thatch and needed the incline to shed rain. As Allen G. Noble points out in *Wood, Brick, & Stone*, good thatching materials were not readily available in North America, so the plentiful forests provided wood shakes, shingles, and planks, making the steep roofs less necessary. However, in Vermont, with its heavy inland snowfalls, roofs to this day remain more steeply pitched on many houses than in other New England states. Also, being close to Quebec, the influx of French Canadians was felt. The Quebec cottages of the eighteenth century often had bell-cast roofs, a relict of cottages in France in which the slightly flattened eaves were a device to throw water away from the clay or earthen walls. Though this was unnecessary in Quebec, where houses were constructed of wood or stone, the style persisted up until the twentieth century.

Of necessity, all the original settlers had to be husbandmen. Land had to be cleared to plant sustaining crops. To this day, forests cover more than 78,000 acres of Vermont's area, and the indigenous trees include pine, hemlock, spruce, fir, sugar maple—Vermont is the country's largest producer of maple syrup—birch, beech, oak, elm, poplar, and many fruit trees. Timber from these forests was used to build houses and furniture, and sawmills were powered by rivers and streams. In addition, Vermont had rich quarries for granite and over a hundred varieties of marble. Vermont marble made mantels and fireplaces that were used all over New England.

Heavy winter snows all over New England prompted the invention of devices that were not necessary in the mother country of England. Barn doors were constructed on rollers so that they could open sideways, close to the side of the barn instead of outward into the snow drifts. The cruel New England winters also caused the origination of the connecting houses and barns that are seen throughout the region. *Big House, Little House, Back House, Barn* by Thomas C. Hubka is a fascinating book that describes these New England farm buildings in detail. This arrangement enabled the farmer to look after his livestock without too much hardship during the bitter cold months.

Though Vermont's population was slow in growing—from the first, isolated trappers to the craftsman-agrarian society of the eighteenth century—the greatest influx into the state has happened since World War II with the proliferating ski and summer resort business. Determined to thwart unscrupulous developers, Vermont passed Act 250 in 1970, a land use law. This was followed by legislation supporting billboard and bottle bans. Overwhelmingly, Vermonters determined not to sell their priceless environmental heritage, and the state, though not wealthy in dollars and cents, is the most richly endowed by nature in all of New England.

Elijah Wright House

A 1792 FARMHOUSE NEAR LAKE CHAMPLAIN

It is not known for certain who built this hipped-roof farmhouse around 1790, but it is similar in both design and plan to four other hipped-roof houses constructed during the same period by Job Lane Howe, a Shoreham builder of note (LEFT). Much of the original glass, rippled with pink and blue tints, remains in the windows.

The long front porch tucked beneath a deep overhang was built off what was the original summer kitchen, and is now the existing kitchen (RIGHT). The windows along the back wall look into the kitchen; the side porch door opens into the dining room.

Much like the eighteenth-century colonists who fled the dense settlements of Massachusetts and Connecticut for the tranquility promised by Vermont, Pat and Chuck Pope came to Shoreham in 1981 from the bustling town of Stockbridge, Massachusetts, in search of a calmer way of life. Located on Lake Champlain, the countryside around Shoreham is a beautiful landscape of rolling mountains and open fields.

The Popes were not interested in working a farm, but they did want a property that embraced several acres—a criterion easily met in the largely agrarian borough of Shoreham, with its large expanses of farmland. Their requisites for a house were similarly simple to satisfy: they wanted a home that would be large enough to accommodate their expanding family of five grown children with spouses and grandchildren during the holidays, but one that could be maintained by just the two of them with little difficulty. The house they decided upon was this hipped-roof farmhouse built for, or by, Elijah Wright around 1790. It is the proverbial rambling farmhouse, which must have sheltered many a large, boisterous family through the years.

Although it is not known precisely who built the house, many believe its builder to be Job Lane Howe, a well-respected craftsman of his day. It is possible, however, that Elijah Wright, its owner, built the house himself, modeling it after those constructed by Job Howe. Elijah apparently did carve his initials, E. W., into one of the closet

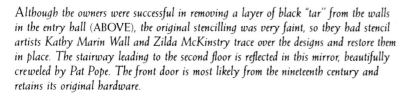

Although the owners were successful in removing a layer of black "tar" from the walls in the entry hall (ABOVE), the original stencilling was very faint, so they had stencil artists Kathy Marin Wall and Zilda McKinstry trace over the designs and restore them in place. The stairway leading to the second floor is reflected in this mirror, beautifully creweled by Pat Pope. The front door is most likely from the nineteenth century and retains its original hardware.

Painted and furnished in classical farmhouse fashion, the dining room (LEFT) is furnished primarily with simple nineteenth-century antiques. The cherry drop-leaf table is a family heirloom and the wrought iron candelabra was made for the room by Vermont blacksmith Leigh Morrell. The walls are white, as they would have been in Elijah Wright's day; the moldings are a shade of green common to colonial interiors. The Parsons box—once used for warming food—is used today as a display niche.

The dining room sideboard (ABOVE) was painted by Pat Pope. The paintings hanging on the wall above are amusing folk-art renderings that depict the owners as they might have looked in the eighteenth century.

doorjambs in the kitchen, which used to be the keeping room. The carving is still visible today; but whether he did so to signify that he was the builder of the house or simply to indicate his ownership has never been ascertained.

Elijah Wright was a figure of some prominence in Shoreham; not only was he among those who firmly established a settlement there, he was also instrumental in the development of Shoreham's sheep-breeding pursuits, which provided substantial revenue for the community.

The town of Shoreham was chartered in 1761 by New Hampshire Governor Benning Wentworth, and in 1766, under the leadership of Colonel Ephraim Doolittle, a small settlement was organized by a group of eleven men. This band of eleven built a simple log house in which they lived communally while they cleared the surrounding land from which they intended to carve their individual farms. However, the state of New York laid claim to the land, and so discouraged were these first settlers by this claim that, with the exception of one of their members, Paul Moore, they returned to their native Massachusetts. Moore remained alone in Shoreham until 1773, when he was joined by others from Connecticut and Massachusetts to live in the settlement.

Following the spring of 1775, despite the valiant military efforts of Ethan Allen and Benedict Arnold, British invasions into Shoreham and the surrounding area drove everyone but Paul Moore away. Moore did not fare well at the hands of the British; his house was burned, his cattle killed, and he was taken prisoner. Although he escaped from the jail at Crown Point Fort, he was recaptured and imprisoned in Canada. It was not until 1783 that he was able to return to Shoreham and reestablish his farm and rebuild his homestead.

By 1785, after the threats of British intrusion and land claims leveled against Shoreham by adjoining colonies had subsided, the settlement at Shoreham finally and firmly took root. The community witnessed tremendous growth between 1786 and 1800, and among those who settled there during that period was Elijah Wright, who had come from Ticonderoga, New York.

Elijah Wright's house has survived the past two centuries relatively unscathed. The structure has been updated with modern mechanical systems, and some refurbishment—most of it cosmetic—has been necessary. Around 1830 the central chimney and all the fireplaces throughout the house were replaced with woodburning stoves. Yet, for the most part, the large white farmhouse has changed little through the years and, aside from some additions, remains true to its eighteenth-century design and layout.

The front door opens into a small entry, which leads to the living room on the left and the dining room on the right. The master bedroom and bath, which are adjacent to the living room in the rear portion of the house, occupy the space that was probably the original kitchen. The existing kitchen, which adjoins the dining room along the front of the house, was once the summer kitchen. The family room is also located in the front segment of the house and is open to the kitchen; this room was most probably a woodshed when the house was first built. The six-room apartment located behind the fam-

This charming blue and white bedroom displays a spool bed—also called a rope bed because ropes were strung through holes in the wood to hold the feather mattress—and a small desk, both nineteenth-century pieces. The wooden circus figures belonged to Chuck Pope when he was a boy.

Situated just off the dining room, the master bedroom (ABOVE) occupies the space believed to have been the original kitchen or keeping room. Until 1830 or 1840, this room contained a commodious fireplace, which, along with all the others in the house, was completely removed because woodburning stoves were more efficient. At that time, homeowners were taxed according to the number of fireplaces they had.

192

ily room in the rear of the house was added sometime before 1820, and it, too, remains substantially unaltered. The second floor is comprised of four bedrooms and a bath, which was once a small bedroom.

Although the upkeep of the house demands the Popes' constant attention, most of their efforts have just been decorative and cosmetic. They have removed old wallpaper, done some replastering, made the baths more livable—but haven't had to do anything thus far that involves actual structural work.

Perhaps the most rewarding aspect of the Popes' refurbishment has been the restoration of the original stencilling discovered beneath layers of old wall covering—certainly one of the most historically unique features of the house. The stencil work found in the gray guest room and other stencilled rooms has been identified as the work of

the Border Man, an itinerant artist—name unknown—who stencilled designs in homes throughout New England during the nineteenth century; he was so named because he limited his designs to the borders of a room. The stencilling in this room is original, and has been restored where necessary due to fading and deteriation. One small wall was left untouched. Vermont stencil artists Kathy Marin Wall and Zilda McKinstry restored the patterns and colors of the original design on the remaining walls.

The furnishings throughout the house are what one would most likely expect to find in a weathered New England farmhouse. There are simple country antiques in every room as well as a miscellany of family mementos and "artifacts we can't part with for whatever reason," as Pat Pope describes some of the accents and accessories and

Although it retains its unpretentious eighteenth-century appeal, the large farmhouse kitchen (ABOVE) is organized and detailed to streamline the cooking activities of a large family. The gas oven is a recent addition, as are the tile counters and butcherblock counter.

A charming focal point in the kitchen is the antique Weir stove, made in 1912 in Taunton, Massachusetts (RIGHT). The woodburning stove, which still has its original gray enamel finish, is occasionally used, but most often functions as a quaint conversation piece and a display area.

treasured finds. The sideboard in the dining room, for example, was salvaged by one of the Popes' children. Left behind by the previous owner of a house purchased by one of the Popes' daughters and her husband, it was not in the best of shape. All agreed that when painted, the salvaged sideboard would add a decorative focal point to the dining room, and so it was brought to Shoreham where it was hand-painted by Pat Pope.

"We've always emphasized the personal touch in our houses," says Pat Pope, "and it's often an unconscious effort. The personal things—the things that are meaningful to our family—always work themselves in." A delightful case in point is the pair of portraits hung above the dining room sideboard. Painted by well-known folk artist Jeanne Marston, these family treasures are interpretive portraits of Pat and Chuck Pope.

The Popes are less concerned with reconstructing an eighteenth- or nineteenth-century ambience than they are with creating a home in which they feel comfortable. "One of the things these old houses do well is adapt," says Pat Pope. "This was a comfortable farmhouse in its day and it continues to be a comfortable farmhouse now. To some extent, that's a result of the way we've chosen to furnish it, but no matter how the house is furnished by future owners, I'm certain it will remain just as inviting. Old houses such as this one may require more tender loving care than most, but they're worth it."

And just as the Popes have taken care to preserve the character of the house, so, too, have they strived to retain the character of the site. The land on which the house stands has not been farmed for many years and the old granary and barns have long stood vacant. But like the farmhouse, these old structures have survived the passing decades most admirably. It is the Popes' intention to restore the granary and barns one day, although they are somewhat undecided as to how they would put them to use once restored. The restoration is, nonetheless, an endeavor that the Popes feel should be undertaken. "We will certainly never farm this land," says Chuck Pope, "but the farm buildings are an important part of Elijah Wright's legacy. He was a farmer and he worked very hard to build much of what we own here. I think we owe it to him to see that it's preserved for as long as possible."

The owners have focused meticulous attention on the restoration of the original stencilling discovered beneath layers of old wallpaper. The eclectic blend of furnishings in this room comprises antiques acquired by the owners over the course of many years. A spool bed, handmade quilt, and Primitive painting add an eighteenth-century flavor to the New England farmhouse decor.

The old brass crib in this room has been handed down through the owner's family and is frequently used by visiting grandchildren. When the house was originally built, the wood floors were left untreated; while the Popes have restored the natural wood floors in other rooms, they chose this cheerful off-white for the baby's room.

The fireplace wall in this room has been carefully restored and touched up where necessary. When the Border Man painted his designs throughout the house, he used yellow ochre paint on the center panels of the upstairs walls which are still well preserved today. The rural simplicity of the room is enhanced by the beautiful crewelwork chair.

A European antique, this carved cherub (RIGHT) is a whimsical extension of the stencilled walls throughout the house and is one of Pat Pope's most cherished possessions.

Reconstructed Colonial

A 1680 SALTBOX AND AN 1840 GENERAL STORE JOINED IN WINDSOR COUNTY

The large clapboard saltbox that graces fifty wooded acres of Windsor County is an unusual example of New England architecture. The owners had been unable to find the old farmhouse they were looking for, and so set out to reconstruct their own colonial. In colonial times it was not uncommon for houses to be enlarged by adding structures or portions of structures that had been erected on neighboring land and, for whatever reason, were no longer of use to their builder. This house, however, is a total reconstruction, completed only in the last decade, and is not even native to the acreage on which it is now comfortably nestled. The main part of the house, a traditional center-chimney saltbox dating from 1680, was moved from North Kingston, Rhode Island, and the ell extending from it, originally a general store built in 1840, was moved from Royalton, Vermont. In addition, an old weathered barn was moved from Bradford, Vermont.

This reconstructed colonial is the impressive result of a recent development in domestic architecture. The Rhode Island house was found through a preservationist who specializes in the acquisition, dismantling, and moving of old buildings. The 1680 saltbox, located in a slum area, was in a state of decay. Abused over the years, it was slated to be demolished only two weeks before it was rescued by the visionary preservationist. Recognizing the structural integrity of the building, she was able to marshal forces and save the bones of the

The main section of the reconstructed colonial is a center-chimney saltbox dating from 1680 (LEFT). Expanded during the early 1700s, it is a much larger house than most built during the late-seventeenth and early-eighteenth century, indicating its original owner was of substantial means. The basic structural elements of the house were moved to the site from Rhode Island. The cedar-shakes roof, dark-stained clapboards, and wood windows are part of the 1980 reconstruction.

The family's pet chickens, Cleo and Wallace, forage for food in the autumn foliage (RIGHT).

The house is actually two buildings—the main portion is a saltbox dating from 1680, the attached ell was originally a general store. The structures were moved from two separate locations—the saltbox is from North Kingston, Rhode Island, the general store, purchased for only three hundred dollars, is from Royalton, Vermont—and were joined together on an idyllic site in Windsor County.

The barn (BELOW), which was dismantled and moved from Bradford, Vermont, shelters the family's horse and a small brood of chickens.

The pond, located behind the house and forming a natural part of the landscape, was created by the owners when they constructed the house.

The owners' horse, Thankful, at pasture (BELOW).

Although the configuration of the keeping room fireplace is true to the original seventeenth-century design of the center-chimney saltbox, the bricks, though old, are not original to the house. Because it is common practice to package only the main structural elements when a house is moved, the chimney stones were left behind. Fortunately the owners had been collecting old bricks from around the area, and these were used to reconstruct the chimney and fireplaces. The wood panelled walls and small cupboard above the fireplace are elements that were added during the reconstruction.

saltbox that now stands in Windsor County. As in most undertakings of this nature, only the main structural elements were salvaged. Photographs were taken and architectural drawings were made to insure the accuracy of the reconstruction. Crews then dismantled the building and the pieces were carefully numbered and packed up for transport by flatbed truck.

The reconstruction work was a collaborative effort between architect Livingston Elder of Walpole, New Hampshire, and builder Ray Clark of Lyme, New Hampshire. The project began in May of 1980 and was completed eighteen months later; the handsome result is a classic-looking central-chimney saltbox that has all the modern conveniences of a new house: Insulated plaster walls were erected, modern plumbing, heating, and electrical wiring were installed, and space was cleverly created for bathrooms and closets and even a small study.

As the owners had planned eventually to redo an old house, they had, over the years, collected many of the elements necessary for rebuilding the structures they had acquired. For example, old planks of floorboard, doors, hardware, and, most important, bricks were used to replace what either had been lost to the ravages of time or were impossible or impractical to move. The original chimney had to be left behind, and so the eight thousand old bricks the owners had amassed were used to reconstruct the central chimney and five fire-

In the past, newly made bricks were often left uncovered outdoors and thus were often imprinted with children's handprints or animal pawprints. At least one such brick has been incorporated into every fireplace, including this one, which is set into the keeping room hearth (BELOW).

Living and dining area are combined in the keeping room, much as they would have been in colonial times (RIGHT). Dinner is often enjoyed by the light of the fire, which is kept burning all winter long, and which can heat the room to seventy degrees or more. The table, purchased for seven dollars in Canada and refinished by the owner, is set with Herend china and Tiffany silver. A more casual tone is achieved, however, by using French provincial placemats. Thumb-back chairs surround the table.

places. Most of the floors survived, but nearly all of the doors were
missing and needed to be replaced, as did the hardware.

The oldest part of the house, dating from 1680, comprises the
living room and bedroom above it. In the ensuing decades the saltbox
was enlarged to include an additional parlor, front entry hall, and
staircase in the front of the house, a keeping room in the back, and
two bedrooms on the second floor. The keeping room, traditionally
used in colonial times as the primary living area—for cooking, eating, even sleeping—and which is still called the keeping room by the
present owner, was probably added to the structure sometime during
the 1720s and 1730s. In addition, a discovery was made during the
reconstruction process that this room did not fit together neatly with
the rest of the building, prompting the architect to theorize that the
keeping room had been moved from another site rather than built as a
new addition.

The new ell, formerly the general store, was initially intended to
be used as a garage. The beams and floorboards were in such good
condition, however, the owners decided to convert the space into an
office and additional living space. The structure was moved twelve
feet to meet the elevation of the saltbox, and a garage and mud room
were installed underneath the main floor. The main floor of the ell is
comprised of a study and sewing room, and located above is a spacious apartment, used often by the children.

Despite the unconventional nature of this reconstructed house,
the saltbox section in particular reveals fine examples of colonial architecture. The exposed ceiling beams and boards in the living room
and keeping room are characteristic of late-seventeenth- and early-
eighteenth-century construction; additionally, they offer further evidence that the keeping room was not part of the original structure.
The beams in the living room are darker than those in the keeping
room, an indication that the living room—the original main room of
the house—was in fact the room in which the cooking had been done
for many years.

Three of the original panelled chimney breasts survived the
move, and were crucial to the reconstruction process, since the house
was essentially rebuilt to fit the dimensions of these wooden panels.
The panelling, probably added to the house during its expansion in

the 1720s and 1730s, is typical of early colonial fireplaces. The large fireplaces, essential sources of both heat and light in colonial days, are also constructed in characteristic fashion—high, deep, and wide to safely accommodate large fires for cooking and heating.

Today the house works well for the busy, active family that lives there. A cheerful, comfortable country effect is evident throughout the rustic interior. Collections of old wood furniture, much of it acquired from northern Vermont and Canada, and cozy upholstered couches and wing back chairs are complemented by country prints and fabrics, rag and braided rugs, and antique picture frames and prints.

Thoughtful energy also went into landscaping the property and determining where the house should be sited. When the property was purchased, it was a densely wooded tract. Although many acres of woods were retained, the six acres surrounding the house and barn were cleared and the house was carefully oriented to the sun. Each room in the house looks out to views of the surrounding trees; those situated in the rear of the house also look out to the pond that was

The reconstruction of the house began with the central chimney and its fireplaces. The chimney had to be constructed so that the panelled fireplace wall, or chimney breast, and beams would fit it exactly. The rest of the house then fell into place. This chimney breast in the living room was left its natural wood finish (LEFT).

One of the finer pieces in the house is this eighteenth-century walnut chest, which the owners acquired in England. A Richard Ginori soup tureen graces its surface (RIGHT).

The antique horse-and-cart (TOP), was purchased in a New Hampshire antiques shop.

The panelled fireplace wall and exposed beam ceiling in the master bedroom date the structure to the late-seventeenth century. The chairs are early-eighteenth-century; the braided rug is new. Although many of the floors in the house were hand-planed, oiled, and polyurethaned, here they were painted with the Apollo blue color that is used thematically throughout the house (BOTTOM).

added to the property. The barn, moved from Bradford, was positioned to allow the owner to see the animals it houses from her kitchen window, while at the same time to not block the view of the drive. "I loved looking out through this window and watching the children get off of the school bus and walk down the drive to the house. That one small detail has furnished me with some lovely memories."

Clearly the attention to detail and the care and imagination that went into re-creating this colonial will continue to provide its residents with endless pleasure in the years to come.

The eighteenth-century cannonball bed in the master bedroom (ABOVE) is positioned to take advantage of views of the trees. The bed and drop-leaf table are both from the nineteenth century; the side table is late-eighteenth-century. The antique botanical prints were framed by the owner with some of the antique picture frames she collects.

The most significant structural element in the house is the front staircase (LEFT), which has survived through the centuries intact. Staircases were often altered either to update a house or simply because they wore out from normal use. With the exception of some of the balusters, every stair and section of the panelling of this staircase is completely original.

The enclosed stairway leading from the second floor landing to the attic is part of the original panelled staircase. The door still maintains its original hardware (RIGHT).

To lend a bit of interest to wide expanses of planked walls, the owners built in several wall niches in which collectibles are artfully displayed.

NEW HAMPSHIRE

The region that Captain John Mason was to name New Hampshire, after the fertile county in England, was founded in confusion. It remained a territory with uncertain boundaries until the latter part of the eighteenth century.

English explorer Martin Pring anchored in Piscataqua harbor, close to present-day Portsmouth, in 1603. Samuel de Champlain sailed along the comparatively short coastline of New Hampshire two years later and discovered the Isles of Shoals eight miles off the mainland—today the islands are divided between New Hampshire and Maine. The famous English adventurer Captain John Smith (1580–1631), cofounder of Jamestown, Virginia, came to the New World on a second visit to map the coast of New England. He visited the Piscataqua harbor and some of the hinterlands of the surrounding area, returning home to write *A Description of New England* in 1616. A group from Cape Cod under the leadership of David Thompson settled at Little Harbor (now Rye), but there is little record of this colony. Around the same time there were settlements at Dover, and at Strawberry Bank (now the site of a restoration near Portsmouth). A permanent community was started at Exeter, according to Oscar Theodore Barck, Jr. and Hugh Talmage Lefler in *Colonial America*, in 1638 by the Reverend John Wheelwright and about thirty-five other exiled supporters of religious reformer Anne Hutchinson. Hampton was settled shortly after by Orthodox Puritans from Massachusetts.

Meanwhile the Maine-Hampshire region had been granted to two Englishmen, Sir Ferdinando Gorges and Captain John Mason, by the Council for New England, set up by James I. The two men reached an agreement in 1629 whereby the land from the Kennebec River to the Piscataqua River went to Gorges (Maine) and the land to the south and west to Mason (New Hampshire). The same year, Massachusetts received a grant for more or less the same territory. John Mason had wanted to establish a semifeudal domain based on the fur trade, and issued a welter of land grants with confusing

boundaries. This caused the land to fill slowly. Settlements that did sprout up over the state were independent and lacked a central government. Eventually New Hampshire was declared a royal province and the boundaries were resolved in 1764.

Society was slow to develop and most families, subsisting on independent farming, lived in simple houses until the mid-1700s. The Granite State, with its thin soil, was no match for Vermont's fertile land, and the meager coastline could not compete with Maine's sea harvests. But New Hampshire produced strong fighting men who served well in the Revolutionary War, and indeed, in every war since. The state motto is aptly Live free or die.

Some of the earliest houses may have been influenced by the settlers from the Cape Cod area. It was in this peninsula that a derivation of a common English cottage was born. The Cape Cod cottage is a simple, almost square house with the typical early colonial massive central chimney. The interior divides into three rooms, and the chimney provides three hearths—two for heating the two equal-sized rooms, and one for heating and cooking in the longer kitchen area. The roofs of these houses were sharply angled, at about forty-five degrees, with the eaves almost touching the top of the ground floor windows. This provided a very small upper floor. The structure sat low and square to the ground, hugging the landscape, which suited areas of high winds and raw winters. As with all early New England houses, these were constructed from timber frames held together with oak pegs in mortise-and-tenon joints, with narrow clapboards, and simple, unornamented casement windows. As New Hampshire gradually filled up, larger and more sophisticated houses began to be built using the state's rich timber.

Craftsmen and furniture makers started to ply their trades toward the end of the eighteenth century, producing pieces that rivaled those of the more fashionable and advanced states. Dining room furniture of mahogany and satinwood made by New Hampshire craftsman Stephen Adams is as much admired today as it was in 1778. Stratford's Samuel Blake was a skilled craftsman, and his furniture is still treasured in that town. John Gaines III (1704–1743) of Portsmouth made outstanding furniture, much of it still in the family (as well as pieces in the Metropolitan Museum of Art in New York City). He designed the "Portsmouth type of baluster," and nearly every important house in Portsmouth has his identical design in its main staircase. This included three uprights to a step; one turned, one spiraled, and one fluted. Langley Boardman (1760–1829), also of

Portsmouth, owned an important workshop at 3 Congress Street that employed many workmen and apprentices. He designed and built his own house, which is one of the most beautiful in the town. Using the Sheraton and Hepplewhite styles as inspiration, Boardman designed several sets of chairs, a mahogany sofa, and an early Empire sideboard that still exist in his house. Added to which, Langley Boardman held several public offices in Portsmouth, including that of state senator.

The increasing sophistication of New Hampshire society can be gleaned from studying the Matthew Harvey House in this section. Though a farmhouse, the second floor sports a ballroom, albeit small and countrified. And the Parsonage in Hollis with its extensive renovations has brought a refreshing and discerning new life to the 1811 structure.

New Hampshire itself is currently going through a period of remodeling. The past two decades have brought an influx of outsiders to the state, lured by low taxes and a pro-business climate. The state has become a center for high-technology magazine publishing and mail order industries, which are as modern as the solar heating at the Peabody's Parsonage. Finding such a positive balance between the old and the new as is seen at the house in Hollis would be a worthwhile goal for this rapidly changing state.

Matthew Harvey House

A 1784 WHITE CLAPBOARD NEAR THE SUNAPEE MOUNTAINS

Two centuries have passed since Matthew Harvey built his farmhouse in central New Hampshire, but the house and its surrounding 250 acres of woods and fields have weathered time's passage most admirably. Today, the farm appears much as it did when Matthew Harvey and his descendants still claimed it as their own.

Certainly, this homestead has seen its share of change through the years; like most New England houses that have sheltered successive generations, this one, too, bears evidence of renovation and growth. The fields surrounding the house have had to be cleared in recent years of the heavy undergrowth born of decades long past. But the farm has always enjoyed the guardianship of loving owners and even now would most assuredly make Matthew Harvey proud.

Matthew Harvey came to New Hampshire from Massachusetts, and though his name may not be recorded in important history textbooks, he played a leading role in the founding and development of this part of central New Hampshire in about 1780. The house was built in 1784, but it is thought that originally it was simply one large room with a sleeping loft incorporated above. A one-room house would have been somewhat unusual at that time because, though most early New England homes were constructed as single-room dwellings, those built in the latter part of the seventeenth century and beyond were typically larger. It's conceivable, however, that lacking the funds

The hand-carved exterior shutters, which sheltered colonial interiors from the bitter New England winter winds, are still functional (LEFT).

The house that Matthew Harvey built more than 200 years ago proffers a proud countenance to the New Hampshire community he helped to establish (RIGHT). The central-chimney house is distinguished by a gabled silhouette, wooden construction, a simple two-story plan, and the clapboard siding that became the hallmark of colonial New England design.

The spring house (NEAR RIGHT) situated on the north end of the property, was purchased by the owner from the Bradford Springs Hotel in Bradford, New Hampshire. The small octagonal building contained the pump from which visitors at the hotel could drink the water believed to contain medicinal qualities. The interior walls are covered with the carved initials and dates of many who visited there.

to erect a more spacious house, Matthew Harvey simply started small.

Some suggest that the house may have been built as a tavern, but the present owner's research indicates that it did not become a tavern until the mid-nineteenth century and that, while the house did indeed function as such, it was always maintained as a private home. Many houses doubled as taverns, but all they really amounted to was a convenient place for a traveler to stop for a meal or overnight lodging. The town records indicate that the original owner's son, Jonathan Harvey, owned a liquor license for the house. The current owner's theory is that the large room off the garage is the original house, because it has a separate frame and because the partition dividing this room from the rest of the house is unusually thick, hinting that it once was an exterior wall. It is very likely that this one room was everything—sitting room, dining room, and kitchen (it has a large fireplace with a cooking stove and bake oven). As the Harvey family acquired the money and time, they were able to enlarge the house. By the time Jonathan Harvey had gained ownership of the property in the early-nineteenth century, the house had assumed its present size.

Like many houses in the area, this one is a simple, but sturdy New England farmhouse. In rural New England, wood was the most common building material, and clapboard siding was used for the exterior sheathing. The interior finishing and detailing were also in character with what were essentially the houses of unpretentious, hardworking people.

Although this house certainly reflects the simplicity of the rural

A nearby fairground gave this structure to the owner (RIGHT). It is believed to have been the ticket booth and executive office at the entrance to the now-defunct fairground.

223

countryside, it is in some respects more elaborate than its simple facade would suggest. The second floor ballroom, for example, is hardly a typical feature of New England farmhouses. Although ballrooms were incorporated into some early New England dwellings, they were almost always confined to houses that also operated taverns. It would have been a rare New England farmer who would devote precious square footage to a room so infrequently—and rather impractically—used.

But Jonathan Harvey, by all accounts, was a prominent figure in New Hampshire, and he apparently designed the house as the setting for a good deal of gracious entertaining. He was, in fact, active politically. At one time or another, he was a representative to Congress, president of the senate of New Hampshire, a selectman, town clerk, a justice of the peace, and an officer in the militia. It is likely that he and his wife entertained quite a bit.

Jonathan Harvey served as adjutant of the Thirtieth New Hampshire Regiment for a number of years and his farm was the scene of the regiment's annual Muster Day exercises throughout the early 1800s. Staged annually by all regiments, the militia's Muster Days were important to New Hampshire communities—as they were to all New England communities—not only because of their military significance, but also because they provided a spectacular form of entertainment.

Participants and spectators began assembling at the Harvey farm the night preceding the Thirtieth Regiment's muster, and in addition to the townspeople who may have traveled many miles to join in the

The antique chair and flax wheel flanking the ballroom fireplace are typical colonial fillips; the collection of old bottles on the mantel is a small sampling of the owner's complete collection (ABOVE).

The front door opens into the original entry hall (FAR BOTTOM LEFT), which is furnished with heirlooms passed down by the owner's family. The exquisite beadwork chair seat was stitched by his grandmother.

A grandfather clock, purchased by the owner's father, sits on the landing of the narrow stairway opposite the front door (LEFT).

225

festivities, the gathering of onlookers invariably included a fair number of itinerant peddlers, showmen, and such, who, in a carnival spirit, made the most of the commercial opportunities that a Muster Day afforded them.

The day itself dawned to find the road to the Harvey farm alive with the color and rhythm of a crowd eagerly anticipating the call to order. When at last Jonathan Harvey, in full regalia, rode his mount onto the clearing in front of his house and issued the command, the long-awaited spectacle of Muster Day commenced. And what a spectacle it must have been! First came the cavalry—one hundred men riding two abreast, their scarlet coats and black shakos emblazoned against a September blue sky. Next onto the field were the grenadiers, also uniformed in scarlet coats and black shakos, but clad in white

pants in subtle counterpoint to the cavalry's buff. Several companies of riflemen followed the grenadiers—attired like backwoodsmen— and at the rear marched the infantry, carrying arms and equipment, but dressed in civilian garb.

When all had assembled, musicians from each company were called out to form the regimental band that performed under the direction of the drum major. Then, following the chaplain's invocation, the inspector general and field officers advanced to observe drills and carry out their lengthy inspection. Upon completion of the inspection, the men were dismissed for dinner, which was followed by the Grand Review, a military parade considered by most observers to be the highlight of the day's events.

Muster Day, of course, was as much a social occasion as a mili-

tary one, and Jonathan Harvey also hosted the evening's Muster Ball at which officers and their wives mingled with local society in the Harveys' ballroom. To stand in this ballroom today, however, is to know that those were indeed simpler times. Not only is the room much smaller than one might expect, it also seems rather rustic given the purpose for which it was designed. The floor and lower walls are planked, and the mantel, the moldings, and the built-in benches that border the room are executed quite simply. Today the ballroom serves as a guest room: "I don't have much use for a ballroom," says the owner with a smile. Yet having maintained its structural integrity over the years, the ballroom, as it is still called, is an intriguing vestige of the Harvey legacy.

Other vestiges of the Harvey family can be found in the house—

Furnished with elegance and simplicity, the living room where the Harveys frequently entertained is appointed with antiques that belonged to the present owner's family (LEFT and ABOVE). (Even the portraits on the wall are of his forebears.) Although the ambience is colonial, the pieces represent several periods and styles, chronicling, in a sense, the history of the house from the eighteenth to the twentieth centuries. The woodwork is simpler in design and finish than that of the dining room. The wallpaper is not original to the room but was reproduced by the Society for the Preservation of New England Antiquities from an eighteenth-century wall covering the owner found in Middlebury, Vermont.

The small rolltop desk in the living room (LEFT) is thought to be an early-twentieth-century piece but seems an appropriate addition to the room scheme. One of the owner's prized possessions is Jonathan Harvey's journal, shown here on the desk. The journal, acquired by sheer luck, bears Jonathan Harvey's signature on the front cover and contains a detailed accounting of the goings-on in the house from April 21, 1823, to November 27, 1861.

While most of the furnishings are rather simply executed, this sofa (BELOW and RIGHT) is beautifully carved—embellishment born of the new yearning for elegance that ushered in the nineteenth century.

Perhaps the most elegant room in the house is the dining room (TOP). The nineteenth-century Hitchock dining chairs still display their original painted finish. The wallpaper was reproduced by the Society for the Preservation of New England Antiquities from remnants discovered on the walls by the present owner.

The sterling silver tea service (MIDDLE) was purchased by the owner's father at Arts and Crafts of Boston.

Resting elegantly on a sterling silver tray is a family heirloom—a pedastalled crystal fruit bowl (BOTTOM).

230

In researching the original structural detailing of the house, the owner's family discovered that the dining room included a corner cabinet, which was missing at the time they purchased the house. A local cabinetmaker constructed the piece, but the owner's mother—a woman quite gifted artistically—carved the shell niche (LEFT).

The raised panelling in the dining room—all of which is original—reflects the elegant Georgian influence that made its appearance in colonial architecture in the early-eighteenth century (LEFT).

for example, several pieces of Harvey furnishings have remained; however, the current owner has resided here for fifty years and thus has added a significant chapter to its history. Although he did not grow up in the house, it has been home to him from the time he was twenty-one. His family purchased the farm from a granddaughter of Jonathan Harvey's sister, Marian McCollum, and though they were the first owners not descended from Matthew Harvey, the family respected and nurtured the rich tradition that the Harveys established. The farm is maintained as a working farm and the house as the simple farmhouse it has always been.

It has, of course, been necessary to make improvements from time to time. The kitchen, for example, was enlarged and updated by the present owner in the interest of modern convenience. Shaped from space once occupied by the old kitchen and a small pantry, the new kitchen was designed in an open plan that melds it with the informal living area that was probably once a large keeping room.

But while the colonial simplicity of the house has been carefully preserved, this is most definitely not a museum-like home; the house with its warm colors and rich fabrics is—and feels—very much lived in. And though it does indeed bear the distinct imprint of its past, it also boasts a vitality sparked by the promise of continuity. Most rooms are furnished in a nineteenth-century vernacular; but filled with the owner's heirlooms, collections, and personal mementos, they speak as clearly of him and of his family as they do of the Harveys.

231

Parsonage

A STATELY 1811 WOOD AND BRICK FEDERAL HOUSE IN HOLLIS

The *Parsonage, a Federal style house built in 1811, features a clapboard facade and, because of the two chimneys, brick sides. The elliptical fanlight over the front door is another hallmark of houses built during this period (LEFT).*

It was not uncommon for houses of the late-eighteenth and early-nineteenth centuries to have clapboard front and rear facades and brick sides (RIGHT). In the restoration the bricks were cleaned by hand and all exterior shutters were repaired or restored. The new historically-styled six-over-six windows are double glazed to provide superior insulation.

Originally a four-room house, The Parsonage was built in 1811 by Esther Frothingham Emerson, the widow of the Reverend Daniel Emerson III. Even though her husband died before the house was finished, she still brought her family from Dartmouth, Massachusetts, to live in the town of Hollis. The house, expanded and altered over the years, had always been used as a parsonage for Hollis until the present owners purchased it in 1979.

Founded in 1730, Hollis was, by 1811, a prosperous farming community. Set amidst verdant fields and lush, rolling hills, Hollis had been chiseled from the Massachusetts township of Dunstable. Until the mid-eighteenth century, Dunstable comprised an area that now includes the towns of Hollis, Pepperell, Brookline, Dracut, Pelham, Townsend, Groton, Londonderry, Merrimack, Milford, Amherst, Litchfield, Hudson, Tyngsborough, Dunstable, and Nashua—communities that now occupy the states of Massachusetts and New Hampshire.

Massachusetts and New Hampshire engaged in a bitter controversy over possession of this territory and the boundary lines that defined it. As Abbie C. Burge, a local historian, wrote in *Hollis, An Agricultural Town*, published in 1898: "Massachusetts was determined to possess all of its fair acres, and New Hampshire had little idea of relinquishing the hard-earned homes and embryo farms of the set-

A latticework breezeway (LEFT) links the house with the garage and also shields the patio from views of the street. Throughout the summer months the cupola on the roof of the rear wing expels warm air and draws cool air into the house through vents recessed in the greenhouse floor below.

The front entry hall (BELOW), which opens into both the living room and the library, incorporates painted pieces. The cabinet is actually an ordinary modern piece that the owner had decoratively painted, as she did the French chairs. The water bucket hanging here is dated 1783 and bears the name Joseph Peabody, Governor Peabody's great-great-great-grandfather.

tlers, to the greed of the Bay colony. Consequently, these sister provinces offered great inducements to influence immigration to this particular locality, each hoping in the end to 'bag the game.'

"The result was that the lands in this region were, for a few years, rapidly taken up, not by trappers and adventurers, but by strong, resolute, and honorable men—men who came for a purpose, and that purpose to make for themselves and their families, comfortable homes, to convert the forests into fruitful farms, and to educate their children."

In 1739 the Massachusetts government formed a separate district from the western sector of Dunstable, naming it simply West Dunstable. In 1741 West Dunstable became a part of New Hampshire, and in

The two-story greenhouse extends the full length of the new rear addition and provides much of the heat for the house during the winter and the cooling in summer months. Warm air from the greenhouse is conducted by thermostatically controlled fans up into the second floor rooms, which open into the greenhouse through sliding windows and doors. Excess heat is stored in the living area adjoining the greenhouse and can be circulated through the house via a second fan system. The rear wing is well insulated and solar heat is more than sufficient to heat it on a cold winter day. At night the Peabodys rely on a Vermont Casting Resolute stove, and when they are away, on backup oil heat.

1746 Governor Wentworth of New Hampshire rechristened the town Holles, apparently in honor of Thomas Pelham Holles, the Duke of New Castle, and a man by whose hands Governor Wentworth reportedly had obtained his position. Historians are uncertain, however, whether it was for the Duke of New Castle—who, some contend, spelled his name Hollis not Holles—or for Thomas Hollis, a benefactor of Harvard, that Hollis was actually named.

In any event, Hollis became a township of New Hampshire—a thriving one at that—and it was to this flourishing community that Esther Emerson came to establish her new home. Her house on Main Street was subsequently purchased by David Sawtelle in 1836 or 1837 and sold by him in 1851 or 1852 to the Congregational Church, the

only church in Hollis at the time, as a parsonage, which it remained through the 1970s. In 1979 the Congregational Church of Hollis put the house, by then in dire need of restoration, on the market.

When former Massachusetts Governor Endicott Peabody and his wife Toni returned to New England and after living for many years in Washington, D.C., they began to search for a house in Hollis, where they had been frequent visitors. Toni Peabody says that almost from the moment she walked into The Parsonage in 1981 she knew it was the house they wanted. She and her husband purchased the house shortly thereafter and commenced with plans to rejuvenate it.

Although they recognize and appreciate the historic value of the house, the Peabodys embrace the philosophy that even historic

235

Furnishings throughout the house comprise both family heirlooms and pieces the Peabodys have acquired on their own through the years. Against one wall of the living room (ABOVE) is placed a significant Peabody heirloom—a Louis XIV marquetry table. The portraits above the table are of Governor Peabody's great-great-great-grandfather, Joseph Peabody, and of Joseph Peabody's daughter-in-law Martha Endicott. The Sheraton side chairs were painted by the owner and the corner cupboard is a French architectural piece painted in several decorative finishes. It contains a collection of nineteenth-century green Fitzhugh porcelains.

The owner has treated the house to a delightful palette of both bold and subdued hues; in the living room (RIGHT), melon tints predominate. The walls appear to be sponge painted but are actually covered with a Brunschwig wallpaper. The chandelier is French, the mirror, Italian, and the owner's portrait is by the American portrait painter William Draper. The small chest to the left of the hearth is a tiny Sheraton chest, the miniature French stool was purchased at an auction.

The library of The Parsonage (LEFT and BELOW) is a comfortable place where family and friends enjoy the fire or a bit of quiet conversation. The bookcases, new to the house, were crafted by the Hollis woodworker Mo Perkins. The sofa fabric is a reproduction fabric copied from a pattern found in Kenmore, a historic house in Fredericksburg, Virginia.

Though perhaps a bit bolder in hue than its colonial predecessors, this green dining room (LEFT) is appropriately furnished and appointed, and exudes an elegant air. All of the furnishings are antiques, but perhaps the most interesting pieces are the twelve Chippendale chairs—only two of which match. The stencilled floor draws its colors from the chintz draperies. The door leading into the new wing is original to the house.

A doorway links the study with the dining room (ABOVE LEFT). Because the study also adjoins the library, guests can easily circulate from room to room.

One of the more inviting rooms in the house is Toni Peabody's study—a vibrant but cozy space often used for entertaining or dining (ABOVE RIGHT). Designed in deep, rich shades of red and blue, this is a personal retreat where family photographs, well-thumbed books, and treasured mementos accumulate. Above and atop the mantel is a collection of statehouse china, made in England.

houses should accomodate the wants and needs of the occupants. Explaining that they wanted to respect the colonial architecture while assigning the house a twentieth-century role, the Peabodys engaged the architect Hank Huber of Peterborough, New Hampshire, to conceive a renovation plan that would accomplish these goals. The architect determined that because the Peabodys felt that the old kitchen wing, added during the Victorian era, was unsightly and in very bad repair, the house would benefit from a new, albeit compatible, wing. The Peabodys also wanted to explore alternatives for heating the house, which consumed 3,000 gallons of fuel during the winter months. Hank Huber's solution was to design a solar wing that would replace the decrepit kitchen ell and provide heating and cooling for the entire house. The new addition incorporates a kitchen, a family room, two bedrooms, and a two-story greenhouse that heats the house in winter and cools it in summer.

There was, however, much more involved in the renovation of The Parsonage than the addition of a new rear wing. Major repairs had to be completed before many of the architectural revisions could be implemented. Water leaks had caused considerable damage—one wall, in fact, had sunk eight inches as a consequence—the floors and woodwork demanded restoration, and interior walls needed resurfacing. Additionally, the clapboards required replacing, and the old bricks, layered with paint, had to be cleaned by hand rather than by sandblasting because of their delicate composition. And finally, new insulation and double-glazed, historically-styled six-over-six windows were installed and the old shutters repaired.

In terms of architectural style, The Parsonage is typical of New England Federal style houses built right after the Revolutionary War. While New England's early colonial homes were constructed primarily of wood, those built during the late-eighteenth and early-nineteenth centuries were often built, at least in part, of brick, which had become widely available throughout the colonies. The center hall, which divides the living room and library, the original downstairs rooms in Esther Emerson's four-room house, also points to a post-revolutionary war date.

239

There is little information offering the particulars of how The Parsonage grew from four rooms to the substantially larger house it had become by 1979, but the house itself indicated that several remodelings added a number of disjointed elements to the floor plan. Aside from the changes that would be effected by construction of the new wing, the owners and the architect worked out some minor revisions in the layout of the house to better relate the living areas and improve the traffic patterns throughout these rooms. Numerous doors were removed or their location changed, and the wall between the living room and the hall was replaced with an elegant twelve-foot-wide arch.

Just as the Peabodys renovated The Parsonage by adroitly combining past and present, so, too, have they furnished it. The interior design scheme is Toni Peabody's own—elegant, but delightfully uncontrived, successfully blending the old, the new, and the in-between. She uses a vibrant mix of colors and patterns, which she skillfully interlaces with furnishings, including heirlooms as well as serendipitous finds, and creates a comfortable, welcoming effect.

Essentially, the interior design scheme evolved as a blend of what the Peabodys wanted and what the house seemed to require. "I started with a scrapbook full of magazine clippings of rooms, or ideas, or fabrics, or whatever I liked, and took off from there. Of course, no matter how firm your ideas may be or how you may have visualized a room with your mind's eye, there are always alterations to be made once you are actually working in the house. I think that is how a house comes to life."

Among the more distinctive ingredients of this design scheme are the beautiful painted finishes incorporated throughout. Toni Peabody is quite fond of decorative painted finishes and studied for a time at the Isabel O'Neil Studio Workshop in New York. She sponge painted the interior front door of The Parsonage and has painted some of the chairs in the house with decorative finishes. Other students from the O'Neil Workshop were enlisted to execute the finishes on the corner cabinet in the living room and the cabinet and side chair in the entry hall.

The stencilled floor in the dining room—a superb interpretation of a popular colonial art—was executed by Hollis stencil artist Micki Ferland. She researched patterns that would be appropriate for a colonial home of The Parsonage's vintage and chose the colors from the English chintz that had been selected for the draperies. Toni Peabody painted the deep green dining room walls herself one afternoon, completing the job in time for a dinner party that evening.

The woodwork throughout the house was restored or created by Hollis craftsman Mo Perkins and Don Fyfe. They stripped most of the woodwork, which was left its natural color, added the woodwork on the arch linking the living room and entry, built the bookcases in the library and study, and restored many of the shutters.

That The Parsonage has so superbly blended its present with its past and, just as important, looks forward to its future are certainly testimony of the renovation's success. Perhaps more to the point, however, is that it is a tribute to the Peabodys' resolve to make it the comfortable, inviting home they knew it could be.

240

The guest room is called the Bermuda Room because everything in the room belonged to Toni Peabody's father, who raised his family in Bermuda. Located on the second floor of the new solar wing, the room is linked by sliding windows to the upper reaches of the greenhouse. The bed is dressed with antique linens and covered with a quilt in the carpenter's rule pattern. Pierre Deux fabrics are used throughout the room.

SOURCE LIST

Although it is not feasible to furnish a complete source guide, this compendium does provide a representative sampling of suppliers, services, and reading material that those with an interest in New England colonial architecture and interior design will find useful or informative.

Antique

Furnishings,

Art and

Accessories

BECK/ROGERS ANTIQUES
Peachcroft Road
Morristown, NJ 07960
(201) 766-6308
Fine American formal and high-country furniture in its original surfaces; tall clocks, folk art.

CATHERINE BLAIR ANTIQUES, INC.
83 Summit Avenue
Summitt, NJ 07901
(201) 273-5771
Fine eighteenth- and nineteenth-century American and English furniture.

IRVIN AND DOLORES BOYD
Meetinghouse Antiques
509 Bethlehem Pike
Fort Washington, PA 19034
American period and country furniture.

G.K.S. BUSH, INC.
2828 Pennsylvania Avenue, NW
Washington, DC 20007
(202) 965-0653
Specializes in eighteenth-century American furniture.

JUNE AND BEN CARDE
Old Bull House
Main Street
Centerbrook, CT 06409
Pewter, eighteenth-century furniture and accessories.

CAMPBELL HOUSE ANTIQUES
160 E. Doe Run Road
Kennett Square, PA 19348
(215) 347-6756
Specializes in eighteenth- and early-nineteenth-century American furniture.

CLASSICAL AMERICA
P.O. Box 19839
Alexandria, VA 22320
(703) 548-3122
Fine American classical furniture and decorative arts.

MARTIN J. CONLON
P.O. Box 3070
Providence, RI 02906
(401) 831-1810
American antiques and early formal furniture.

KIRT AND ELIZABETH CRUMP
387 Boston Post Road
Madison, CT 06443
(203) 245-7573
Antique clock specialists.

PETER EATON
39 State Street
Newburyport, MA 01950
(617) 465-2754
American furniture in original, as-found condition.

EQUINOX ANTIQUES
Route 7A
P.O. Box 19
Manchester, VT 05254
(802) 362-3540
Specializes in fine eighteenth- and nineteenth-century furnishings and accessories.

EWINGS ANTIQUES
7718 N. Michigan Road
Indianapolis, IN 46268
(317) 299-6074
American country furniture, quilts, folk art, paintings, and accessories of the eighteenth and nineteenth centuries.

FABULOUS THINGS, LTD.
1974 Union Street
San Francisco, CA 94123-4271
(415) 346-0346
Quilts, Americana, folk art.

VIVIAN FARREN
752 La Cienega Boulevard
Los Angeles, CA 90069
(213) 657-6229
American and English furniture, paintings, and period accessories.

FEDERATION ANTIQUES, INC.
2012 Madison Road
Cincinnati, OH 45208
(513) 321-2671
Period and country furniture, fine art, and appropriate accessories.

FOUR CORNERS-EAST ANTIQUES
307 North Street
Bennington, VT 05201
(802) 442-2612
Country and formal American and continental furnishings and accessories.

PATTY GAGARIN ANTIQUES
851 Banks North Road
Fairfield, CT 06430
(203) 259-7332
Early American antiques, folk art, quilts.

ESTELLE M. GLAVEY, INC.
Route 124
New Ipswich, NH 03071
(603) 878-1200
Early American formal and country furniture and accessories.

PAT GUTHMAN ANTIQUES
281 Pequot Avenue
Southport, CT 06490
(203) 259-5743
Antiques and accessories for the kitchen and keeping room.

KENNETH HAMMITT ANTIQUES
Route 6
Woodbury, CT 06798
(203) 263-5676
Fine period and antiques and accessories.

HARMIC'S ANTIQUES GALLERY
U.S. 13 and Route 42
RD 5
Dover, DE 19901
(302) 736-1174
Specialists in Americana.

JOHN HULL INTERIORS/ANTIQUES
Forest Hill
10th at Locust
Boonville, MO 65233
(816) 882-6030
American period furniture and accessories.

NANCY ILIFF ANTIQUES
178 N. Mill Street
Lexington, KY 40508
American furniture and fireplace equipment; eighteenth-century accessories.

DEANNE LEVISON
2995 Lookout Place
Atlanta, GA 30305
(404) 264-0106
American furniture and accessories of the eighteenth and nineteenth centuries.

MARSTON LUCE
1314 21st Street, NW
Washington, DC 20036
(202) 775-9460
Painted furniture, folk art, and quilts.

MARC J. MATZ GALLERY
366-B Broadway
Cambridge, MA 02139
(617) 661-6200
American and English furniture, paintings, and accessories of the seventeenth, eighteenth, and nineteenth centuries.

AUSTIN McDONNELL, INC.
Stevenson Village Center
Baltimore, MD 21153
(301) 484-8466
Fine American and English antiques and accessories.

LYDIA D. PETERS, INC.
RR5
Box 283
North Scituate, RI 02857
(401) 934-1472
American furniture and Americana of the eighteenth century.

PETIT MUSEE
1034 S. Brentwood
Suite 804
St. Louis, MO 63117
(314) 863-2636
American and English decoratives.

C. L. PRICKETT
930 Stony Hill Road
Yardley, PA 19067
(215) 493-4284
Fine American antiques.

QUESTER MARITIME
COLLECTION
P.O. Box 446-Q
Stonington, CT 06378
(203) 535-3860
Marine paintings, prints, nautical instruments, models, furniture, scrimshaw, and sailor-made items.

SHEILA AND EDWIN RIDEOUT
12 Summer Street
Wiscasset, ME 04578
(207) 882-6420
American and English pottery, samplers, and country furniture of the eighteenth and nineteenth centuries.

DONALD R. SACK
P.O. Box 132
Buck Hill Falls, PA 18323
(717) 595-7567
Specializes in American antiques.

SALLEA ANTIQUES
110 Main Street
New Canaan, CT 06840
(203) 972-1050
Fine antique furniture, porcelain, brass, paintings, and boxes.

DAVID A. SCHORSCH, INC.
1037 North Street
Greenwich, CT 06830
(203) 869-8797
Fine Americana.

SCHUELER ANTIQUES
10 High Street
Camden, ME 04843
(207) 236-2770
American furniture, decorative accessories, paintings, and decoys.

BEVERLY KELLER SCOTT
ANTIQUES, INC.
Box 5628
Mission at 7th
Carmel, CA 93921
Antique silver and porcelains.

RON SNYDER ANTIQUES
2011 West Street
Annapolis, MD 21401
(301) 266-5452
Antique furnishings of the eighteenth and nineteenth centuries.

JANICE F. STRAUSS AMERICAN
ANTIQUES
P.O. Box 354
South Salem, New York 10590
(914) 763-5933
American formal and country furniture predating 1840.

TATEWELL GALLERY
Junction Routes 9 and 31
Hillsboro, NH 03244
(603) 478-5755
Early lighting, glass, china, small furniture, fine art, and accessories.

TEMORA PARK ANTIQUES
372 Swamp Road
Newtown, PA 18940
(215) 860-2742
American and English furniture of the eighteenth and nineteenth centuries.

THE ANTIQUES CENTER AT
HARTLAND, VERMONT
Route 5
Hartland, VT 05048
(802) 436-2441
Antiques of the eighteenth and nineteenth centuries offered by more than fifty dealers.

THE BLUE CANDLESTICK
14320 S. Saratoga-Sunnyvale Road
Saratoga, CA 95070
(408) 867-3658
American period and country furniture, spongeware, samplers.

THE HARVEST MILL
40 Parish Street
Canandaigna, NY 14424
(716) 394-5907
Antique period and country furniture and accessories.

THE SILVER VAULT
122 West Main Street
Barrington, IL 60010
(312) 381-3101
American and English silver, brass, copper, and pewter.

Custom-Made Reproduction Furniture

BIGGS COMPANY
105 E. Grace Street
Richmond, VA 23219
(804) 644-2891
Reproductions of eighteenth-century furniture.

JOHNS CONGDON
CABINETMAKER
RFD 1
Box 350
Moretown, VT 05660
(802) 485-8927
Cabinetwork in period styles; original designs and authentic reproductions; all work handcrafted.

GERALD CURRY—
CABINETMAKER
Pound Hill Road
Union, ME 04862
(207) 785-4633
Specialists in eighteenth-century reproductions.

JAMES LEA—CABINETMAKER
Harkness House
9 West Street
Rockport, ME 04856
(207) 236-3632
Specializes in handcrafted eighteenth-century American master cabinetmakers' furniture.

J. F. ORR AND SONS
215 Boston Post Road
Sudbury, MA 01776
(617) 443-3650
Reproduction New England country furniture.

ELDRED WHEELER
60 Sharp Street
Hingham, MA 02043
(617) 337-5311
Offers pieces from three collections of eighteenth-century reproduction furniture: Abby Aldrich Folk Art Collection, Colonial Williamsburg, and Nantucket Historical Association; also original New England designs.

Architectural Antiques

The following is a listing of architectural salvage companies, all of which stock a wide assortment of antique structural elements.

ARCHITECTURAL ANTIQUES
121 East Sheridan
Oklahoma City, OK 73104
(405) 232-0759

ARCHITECTURAL ANTIQUES
EXCHANGE
709-15 N. Second Street
Philadelphia, PA 19123
(215) 922-3669

ART DIRECTIONS
6120 Delmar Boulevard
St. Louis, MO 63112
(314) 863-1895

BYGONE ERA
ARCHITECTURAL ANTIQUES
4783 Peachtree Road
Atlanta, GA 30341
(404) 458-3016

CANAL CO.
1612 14th Street, NW
Washington, DC 20009
(202) 234-6637

GARGOYULES, LTD.
512 South Third Street
Philadelphia, PA 19147
(215) 629-1700

GREAT AMERICAN SALVAGE
CO.
34 Cooper Street
New York, NY 10003
(212) 505-0070

IRREPLACEABLE ARTIFACTS
14 Second Avenue
New York, NY 10003
Showrooms:
14 Second Avenue,
259 Bowery,
1046 Third Avenue
New York, NY 10021

OLDE BOSTONIAN
ARCHITECTURAL ANTIQUES
135 Buttonwood Street
Dorchester, MA 02125
(617) 282-9300

OLDE THEATRE
ARCHITECTURAL SALVAGE
CO.
2045 Broadway
Kansas City, MO 64108
(816) 283-3740

PELNIK WRECKING CO., INC.
1749 Erie Boulevard, East
Syracuse, NY 13210
(315) 472-1031

SALVAGE ONE
1524 S. Sangamon Street
Chicago, IL 60608
(312) 733-0098

THE WRECKING BAR OF
ATLANTA
292 Moreland Avenue, NE
Atlanta, GA 30307
(404) 525-0468

URBAN ARCHAEOLOGY
137 Spring Street
New York, NY 10012
(212) 431-6969

Reproduction

Structural

Components

ARCHITECTURAL
COMPONENTS
P.O. Box 249
Leverett, MA 01054
(413) 367-9441
*Reproduces eighteenth- and nineteenth-
century millwork, doors, window sashes,
and a wide selection of moldings patterned
after those of the Connecticut Valley
architectural style.*

ARCHITECTURAL
MASTERWORKS
3502 Divine Avenue
Chattanooga, TN 37407
(615) 867-3630
*Produces a broad selection of historically
accurate reproduction period architectural
details including friezes, chair rails,
moldings, pilasters, medallions, and doorway
systems.*

ARCHITECTURAL PANELING,
INC.
979 Third Avenue
Suite 1518
New York, NY 10022
(212) 371-9632
*Reproduces paneling, mantels, fireplaces, and
built-in cabinets in wood.*

ARCHITECTURAL
REPRODUCTIONS, INC.
19402 SE Foster
Boring, OR 97009
(503) 658-6400
*Manufacturer and supplier of decorative
architectural elements, which are crafted
from plaster, cast metals, fiberglass, or cast
stone.*

BENDIX MOLDINGS, INC.
235 Pegasus Avenue
Northvale, NJ 07647
(201) 767-8888
*Suppliers of a diverse assortment of
unfinished decorative moldings, carved
ornaments, dentils, crowns, and cornices.*

COLONIAL RESTORATION
PRODUCTS
405 E. Walnut Street
North Wales, PA 19454
(215) 699-3133
*Offers a wide selection of reproduction
components designed for the restoration of
colonial homes. All items are made using
eighteenth-century methods.*

COLONIAL WOODWORKS
P.O. Box 10612
Raleigh, NC 27605
(919) 833-1681
*Specializes in handcrafted mantels in the
Early American style.*

OLD WORLD MOLDING AND
FINISHING CO., INC.
115 Allen Boulevard
Farmingdale, NY 11735
(516) 293-1789
*Moldings, cornices, mantels, and paneling
suited to a variety of architectural periods.*

Restoration

Design and

Consulting

Services

ABBATE AND COMPANY, INC.
1202 Watts Street
Durham, NC 27701
(919) 683-1236
*This firm offers planning and design
presentation, restoration, rehabilitation, and
adaptive services.*

ARCHITECTURAL
PRESERVATION
CONSULTANTS
125 Cedar Street
New York, NY 10006
(212) 227-1271
*Provides such preservation services as
historical research analysis, architectural
surveys, feasibility studies, photographic
documentation, and assistance with national
register nominations.*

ARCHITECTURAL
PRESERVATION TRUST
152 Old Clinton Road
Westbrook, CT 06498
(203) 669-1776
*This firm dismantles, reconstructs, and
restores, seventeenth-, eighteenth-, and
nineteenth-century buildings; stocks recycled
building parts.*

ARCHITECTURAL
RECLAMATION, INC.
312 S. River Street
Franklin, OH 45005
(513) 746-8964
*Provides design and construction of
contemporary structures that are
architecturally compatible with historic
houses; offers contracting services for
restoration, repair, and adaptive reuse.*

HISTORIC PRESERVATION
ALTERNATIVES
15 Sussex Street
Newton, NJ 07860
(201) 579-2525
*Historic research, preservation planning,
historic site surveys, national register
nominations.*

STEPHEN P. MACK
Chase Hill Farm
Ashaway, RI 02804
(401) 377-8041
*An architectural firm that specializes in
dismantling and reassembling eighteenth-
century houses and barns nationwide.*

WILLIAM H. PARSONS AND
ASSOCIATES
420 Salmon Brook
Granby, CT 06035
(203) 653-2281
*Consultants and specialists in preservation
projects.*

PRESERVATION ASSOCIATES,
INC.
207 S. Potomac Street
Hagerstown, MD 21740
(301) 791-7880
*Offer restoration and rehabilitation services
nationwide.*

S.P.N.E.A. CONSERVATION
CENTER
185 Lyman Street
Waltham, MA 02154
(617) 891-1985
*A consulting group of the Society for the
Preservation of New England Antiquities
that offers expert advice to owners of older
homes in the areas of restoration and
preservation.*

TRADITIONAL AMERICAN
    CONCEPTS
1843 Seminole Trail
Charlottesville, VA 22901
(804) 973-3155
*An architectural firm that specializes in
restoration, renovation, reconstruction, or
redesign of period buildings.*

TRADITIONAL LINE, LTD.
143 West 21st Street
New York, NY 10011
(212) 627-3555
*A firm of craftsmen noted for their
commitment to preservation and architectural
conservation; specialists in period
restorations; museum-quality craftsmanship.*

Interior

Finishing,

Design

INTERIOR DECORATIONS
48-52 Lincoln Street
Exeter, NH 03833
(603) 778-0406
*Jane Kent Rockwell specializes in
seventeenth-, eighteenth-, and nineteenth-
century interior decoration throughout New
England.*

BOPAS DECORATIVE ARTS
30 Ipswich Street
Boston, MA 02215
(617) 424-9845
*Artists Gedas Paskaekas and Robert Grady
execute faux finishes including colonial
graining, pickling, and marbleizing and are
also skilled stencil artists.*

JOHN CANNING, ORNAMENTAL
    PAINTER
132 Meeker Road
Southington, CT 06489
(203) 621-2188
*A specialist in executing decorative painted
finishes; services also include restoration and
conservation of historic decoration.*

EVERGREENE PAINTING
    STUDIOS, INC.
365 West 36th Street
New York, NY 10018
(212) 239-1322
*A firm of craftsmen, artists, and designers
who provide such services as conceptual
drawings, the execution of painted finishes
and floorcloths, and the design of custom
wallpapers.*

MACLEAN RESTORATION
    SERVICES
105 Stone House Road
Winchester Center, CT 06094
(203) 738-0048
*Specialists in interior finish restoration;
paints and glazes produced from period
formulae.*

EDWARD K. PERRY CO.
322 Newbury Street
Boston, MA 02115
(617) 536-7873
*Specialists in fine interior and exterior
painting of historic houses.*

WIGGINS BROTHERS
Hale Road
Box 420 Tilton, NH 03276
(603) 286-3046
*Specialists in traditional interior folk
painting, stencilling, murals, and
marbleizing.*

Fabrics and

Wall

Coverings

NANCY BORDEN PERIOD
    TEXTILE REPLICAS
P.O. Box 4381
Portsmouth, NH 03801
(603) 436-4284
*Specializes in museum-documented fabrics of
the seventeenth, eighteenth, and nineteenth
centuries; fabric replications of window
treatments, bed hangings, upholstery; travels
nationwide for in-home consultation.*

BRUNSCHWIG & FILS, INC.
75 Virginia Road
N. White Plains, NY 10603
(914) 684-5800
*Fine reproductions of eighteenth- and
nineteenth-century fabrics and wallpaper.*

COHASSET COLONIALS
643 Ship Street
Cohasset, MA 02025
(617) 383-0110
*Reproduction fabrics, furniture, and
accessories.*

COLONIAL WILLIAMSBURG
    FOUNDATION
P.O. Box C
Williamsburg, VA 23187
(804) 229-1000
*Offers more than 2,000 examples of fine
home furnishings approved by the Colonial
Williamsburg Foundation including fabrics,
wallpapers, and accessories.*

COWTAN AND TOUT, INC.
979 Third Avenue
New York, NY 10022
(212) 753-4488
*Woven and silk fabrics; hand-blocked
wallpapers; custom colorings available.*

CLARENCE HOUSE IMPORTS,
    LTD.
211 East 58th Street
New York, NY 10022
(212) 752-2890
*Reproducers of antique textile designs in fine
fabrics and wall coverings.*

A. L. DIAMENT AND CO.
309 Commerce Drive
Exton, PA 19341
(215) 363-5660
*Extensive line of document wallpapers;
specializes in restoration and does custom
work.*

HINSON AND CO.
979 Third Avenue
New York, NY 10022
(212) 475-4100
*Extensive line of fabrics and wallpaper in a
colonial vein.*

S. AND C. HUBER,
    ACCOUTREMENTS
82 Plants Dam Road
East Lyme, CT 06333
(203) 739-0772
*Produces handcrafted goods of eighteenth-
and nineteenth-century design including
spinning wheels, fibers, handspun yarns, and
fabrics.*

SCALAMANDRE, INC.
950 Third Avenue
New York, NY 10022
(212) 980-3888
*Superb period-design fabrics, wallpapers,
carpets, and trimmings.*

STROHEIM AND ROMANN
155 East 56th Street
New York, NY 10022
(212) 691-0700
Documentary reproduction fabrics.

RICHARD E. THIBAUT, INC.
706 South 21st Street
Irvington, NJ 07111
(201) 399-7888
*Traditional wall coverings and coordinating
fabrics.*

WINTERTHUR MUSEUM AND
    GARDENS
Winterthur, DE 19735
(302) 656-8591
*Reproduction fabrics, wall coverings,
furniture, and accessories.*

Rugs and

Carpets

ADAMS AND SWETT
372 A Dorchester Avenue
Boston, MA 02127
(617) 268-8000
*Braided rugs, rag rugs, hooked rugs, and
others well suited to the colonial interior.*

J. R. BURROWS AND CO.
P.O. Box 418 Cathedral Station
Boston, MA 02118
(617) 451-1982
*Traditional documentary reproduction
carpets.*

COUNTRY BRAID HOUSE
Clark Road
RFD 2, Box 29
Tilton, NH 03276
(603) 286-4511
Specializes in traditional New England colonial braided rugs.

FAMILY HEIR-LOOM WEAVERS
Meadow View Drive
RD3, Box 59 E
Red Lion, PA 17356
(717) 246-2431
Ingrain carpets in historically accurate patterns.

HERITAGE RUGS
P.O. Box 404
Lahaska
Bucks County, PA 18931
(215) 794-7229
Early American rag rugs woven on antique frames; custom orders filled.

PATTERSON, FLYNN AND MARTIN, INC.
950 Third Avenue
New York, NY 10022
(212) 751-6414
Specializes in reproductions of period carpeting; also offers wide selection of needlepoints, and braided and hooked rugs.

STARK CARPET CORP.
979 Third Avenue
New York, NY 10022
(212) 752-9000
Documented carpets for historical restorations; traditional carpets and rugs.

Publications
ANTIQUES AND COLLECTIBLES

AMERICANA
29 West 38th Street
New York, NY 10018
(212) 398-1550
Monthly magazine devoted to American art, antiques, and collectibles.

ANTIQUE MONTHLY
Boone, Inc.
Drawer 2
Tuscaloosa, AL 35402
(205) 345-0272
Monthly tabloid that covers art, antiques, and major museum shows.

ANTIQUE REVIEW
Box 538
Worthington, CT 43085
(614) 885-9757
Monthly tabloid with an emphasis on the history and production of furniture, pottery, china, and other antiques of the periods prior to the 1880s.

ART AND ANTIQUES
89 Fifth Avenue
New York, NY 10003
(212) 206-7050
A glossy magazine published ten times a year that focuses on fine art, antiques, and the decorative arts; also includes listings of gallery and museum shows.

MAINE ANTIQUE DIGEST
P.O. Box 645
Waldoboro, ME 04572
(207) 832-7534
Monthly publication with a focus on early Americana, antique furnishings, nautical artifacts, and folk art.

THE MAGAZINE ANTIQUES
980 Madison Avenue
New York, NY 10021
(212) 734-9797
A monthly magazine that features some of the finest art and antiques available; also includes compendia of exhibitions and auctions both in the United States and abroad.

DECORATING/GARDENING

ARCHITECTURAL DIGEST
5900 Wilshire Boulevard
Los Angeles, CA 90036
(213) 937-4740
Upscale monthly magazine with an emphasis on fine architecture and interior design both in the United States and abroad.

BETTER HOMES AND GARDENS' TRADITIONAL HOME
1716 Locust Street
Des Moines, IA 50336
(515) 284-3000
Quarterly magazine with an emphasis on traditional architecture, gardening, and interior design.

COLONIAL HOMES
1790 Broadway
New York, NY 10019
(212) 830-2900
Bimonthly magazine devoted to coverage of colonial houses both in America and abroad, and of the art, antiques, and collectibles of the colonial era.

COUNTRY HOME
1716 Locust Street
Des Moines, IA 50336
(515) 284-3000
Published ten times a year, this magazine emphasizes the architecture, gardening, decorating, and crafts synonymous with the country and colonial styles.

GARDEN DESIGN, THE FINE ART OF RESIDENTIAL LANDSCAPE ARCHITECTURE
American Society of Landscape Architects
1733 Connecticut Avenue, NW
Washington, DC 20009
(202) 446-7730
Quarterly magazine with a focus on garden history and design. The emphasis is on the design aspects of gardening rather than on the horticultural.

HG
350 Madison Avenue
New York, NY 10017
(212) 880-8800
Monthly house and garden magazine with an emphasis on fine architecture and interior design throughout the world.

HOUSE BEAUTIFUL
1700 Broadway
New York, NY 10019
(212) 903-5000
Monthly magazine that focuses on decorating, architecture, gardening, building and remodeling, and entertaining.

THE WORLD OF INTERIORS
234 Kings Road
London SW3 5VA, England
An elegant monthly magazine that focuses on the very finest architecture and interior design; the emphasis is European, but coverage does include houses in the United States as well.

HISTORY/ RESTORATION/PRESERVATION

AMERICAN HISTORY ILLUSTRATED
Box 8200
Harrisburg, PA 17105
(717) 657-9555
A monthly magazine of cultural, social, military, and political history.

THE OLD-HOUSE JOURNAL
69A Seventh Avenue
Brooklyn, NY 11217
(718) 636-4514
Monthly magazine that provides information and guidance on the restoration and maintenance of houses built prior to 1939.

PRESERVATION NEWS
National Trust for Historic Preservation
1785 Massachusetts Avenue, NW
Washington, DC 20016
(202) 673-4075
A monthly tabloid that presents information concerning historic buildings throughout the United States.

BIBLIOGRAPHY

Books

Albion, Robert G. et al. *New England and the Sea.* Brenington, Marion V., ed. Middletown, Conn.: Wesleyan University Press, 1972.

Barck, Oscar Theodore, Jr., and Lefler, Hugh Talmage. *Colonial America.* New York: Macmillan Publishing Co., 1968.

Bjerkoe, Ethel Hall. *The Cabinetmakers of America.* New York: Doubleday & Co., Inc., 1952.

Bridenbaugh, Carl. *Cities in the Wilderness: The First Century of Urban Life in America, 1625–1742.* London, Oxford, New York: Oxford University Press, 1971.

Bridenbaugh, Carl. *The Colonial Craftsman.* New York: New York University Press, 1950.

Brooks, Van Wyck. *The Flowering of New England.* New York: E.P. Dutton & Co., 1936, 1952.

Bruce, Curt, and Grossman, Jill. *Revelations of New England Architecture.* New York: Grossman Publishers, 1975.

Burchard, John, and Bush-Brown, Albert. *The Architecture of America: A Social and Cultural History.* Boston: Little, Brown & Co., 1961.

Chamberlain, Samuel. *Beyond New England Thresholds.* New York: Hastings House, 1937.

Comstock, Helen. *American Furniture: Seventeenth, Eighteenth and Nineteenth Century Styles.* New York: Viking Press, 1962.

Congdon, Herbert Wheaton. *Early American Homes for Today: A Treasury of Decorative Details and Restoration Procedures.* Rutland, Vt.: Charles E. Tuttle Co., 1963.

Cooper, Wendy. *In Praise of America.* New York: Alfred A. Knopf, 1980.

Delaney, Edmund. *The Connecticut River: New England's Historic Waterway.* Chester, Conn.: The Globe Pequot Press, 1973.

Demos, John. *Remarkable Provinces 1600–1760.* New York: George Braziller, 1972.

Downing, Antoinette F., and Scully, V.J., Jr. *The Architectural Heritage of Newport, Rhode Island: 1640–1915,* 2nd edition. New York: Clarkson N. Potter, 1970.

Eberlein, Harold Donaldson. *The Architecture of Colonial America.* Boston: Little, Brown & Co., 1921.

Fisher, Dorothy Canfield. *Vermont Tradition: The Biography of an Outlook on Life.* Boston: Little, Brown & Co., 1953.

Fitch, James Marston. *American Building: The Historical Forces That Shaped It.* Boston: Houghton-Mifflin Co., 1947.

Fitzgerald, Oscar P. *Three Centuries of American Furniture.* Englewood Cliffs, N.J.: Prentice-Hall Press, 1982.

Foley, Mary Mix. *The American House.* New York: Harper Colophon Books, 1980.

Furnas, J.C. *The Americans: A Social History, 1587–1914.* New York: G.P. Putnam's Sons, 1971.

Gould, Mary Earle. *The Early American House: Household Life In America 1620–1850.* Rutland, Vt.: Charles E. Tuttle, Co., Inc., 1965.

Grant, Ellsworth S. *Yankee Dreamers and Doers.* Chester, Conn.: The Pequot Press, 1973.

Haas, Irvin. *America's Historic Houses and Restorations.* New York: Castle Books, 1966.

Hamlin, Talbot. *Greek Revival Architecture in America.* New York: Dover Publications, 1964.

Hansen, Hans Jürgen, ed. *Architecture in Wood: A History of Wood Building and Its Techniques in Europe and North America.* New York: The Viking Press, 1971.

Hawke, David. *The Colonial Experience.* New York: Bobbs-Merrill Co., 1966.

Hollis History Committee. *Where the Past Has Been Preserved: Hollis, New Hampshire 1819–1979.* Canaan, N.H.: Phoenix Publishing, 1980.

Hunt, William Dudley, Jr. *American Architecture: A Field Guide to the Most Important Examples.* New York: Harper and Row Publishers, 1984.

Hunt, William Dudley, Jr. *Encyclopedia of American Architecture.* New York: McGraw-Hill, Inc., 1980.

Isham, Norman Morrison. *Early American Houses and A Glossary of Colonial Architectural Terms,* 2 volumes. New York: Da Capo Press, 1967.

Jorgensen, Neil. *A Guide to New England's Landscape.* Chester, Conn.: The Pequot Press, 1977.

Kelly, J. Frederick. *Early Domestic Architecture of Connecticut.* New York: Dover Publications, 1955.

Ketchum, William C., Jr. Volume 2 of *The Knopf Collectors' Guides to American Antiques: Furniture, Chests, Cupboards, Desks & Other Pieces.* New York: Alfred A. Knopf, 1982.

Kettell, Russell Hawkes, ed. *Early American Rooms.* Portland, Me.: The Southworth Anthoensen Press, 1936.

Kimball, Fiske. *Domestic Architecture of the American Colonies and of the Early Republic.* New York: Dover Publications, 1950.

Klein, Marilyn W., and Fogle, David P. *Clues to American Architecture.* Washington, D.C.: Starrhill Press, 1985.

Le Grice, Lyn. *The Art of Stencilling.* New York: Clarkson N. Potter, 1986.

Litchfield, Michael. *Renovation: A Complete Guide.* New York: John Wiley & Sons, Inc., 1982.

Lockwood, Luke Vincent. *Colonial Furniture in America,* volumes 1 and 2. New York: Charles Scribner's Sons, 1913.

Madigan, Mary Jean, and Colgan, Susan. *Early American Furniture From Settlement to City.* New York: Billboard Publications, Inc., An Art and Antiques Book, 1983.

McAlester, Virginia and Lee. *A Field Guide to American Houses.* New York: Alfred A. Knopf, 1984.

McManis, Douglas R. *Colonial New England.* New York: Oxford University Press, 1975.

Miller, Edgar G., Jr. *American Antique Furniture.* New York: Dover Publications, 1966.

Morison, Samuel Eliot. *The Maritime History of Massachusetts, 1783–1860.* Boston: Houghton-Mifflin Co., 1961.

Mumford, Lewis. *Sticks and Stones: A Study of American Architecture and Civilization.* New York: Dover Publications, 1955.

Noble, Allen G. *Wood, Brick, & Stone: The North American Settlement Landscape.* Amherst: University of Massachusetts Press, 1984.

Nutting, Wallace. *Furniture Treasury.* New York: The Macmillan Publishing Co., 1963.

Peterson, Harold L. *American Interiors: From Colonial Times to the Late Victorians.* New York: Charles Scribner's Sons, 1971.

Pierce, Neal R. *The New England States.* New York: W.W. Norton and Co., Inc., 1976.

Pratt, Dorothy and Richard. *A Guide to Early American Homes: North.* New York: McGraw-Hill Book Co., 1956.

Rifkind, Carole. *A Field Guide to American Architecture.* New York: New American Library, 1980.

Rogers, Meyric R. *American Interior Design: The Traditions and Development of Domestic Design From Colonial Times to the Present.* New York: Bonanza Books, 1978.

Schwartz, Marvin D. Volume 1 of *The Knopf Collectors' Guides to American Antiques: Chairs, Tables, Sofas, Beds.* New York: Alfred A. Knopf, 1982.

Sedgwick, Sarah Cabot, and Marquand, Christina Sedgwick. *Stockbridge 1789–1839: A Chronicle.* Great Barrington, Mass.: The Berkshire Courier, 1939.

Shea, John G. *Antique Country Furniture of North America.* New York: Van Nostrand Reinholdt, 1975.

Sinnott, Edmund W. *Meetinghouse and Church in Early New England: The Puritan Tradition as Reflected in Their Architecture, History, Builders, and Ministers.* New York: McGraw-Hill Book Co., 1963.

Stern, Robert A.M. *Pride of Place: Building the American Dream*. New York: American Heritage; Boston: Houghton-Mifflin Co., 1986.

Stilgoe, John R. *Common Landscape of America: 1580–1845*. New Haven: Yale University Press, 1982.

Stone, Anne. *Antique Furniture*. New York: Exeter Books, 1982.

Summerson, John. *The Classical Language of Architecture*. Cambridge, Mass.: M.I.T. Press, 1963.

Upton, Dell. *America's Architectural Roots: Ethnic Groups That Built America*. Washington, D.C.: The Preservation Press, 1986.

Verrill, A. Hyatt. *The Heart of Old New England*. New York: Dodd, Mead & Co., 1986.

Walker, Lester. *American Shelter: An Illustrated Encyclopedia of the American Home*. Woodstock, N.Y.: Overlook Press, 1981.

Wertenbaker, Thomas Jefferson. *Puritan Oligarchy: The Founding of American Civilization*. New York: Charles Scribner's Sons, 1947.

Whiffen, Marcus, and Koeper, Frederick. *American Architecture 1607–1976*. Cambridge, Mass.: M.I.T. Press, 1981.

Williams, Henry L., and Williams, Ottaliek. *A Guide to Old American Houses, 1700–1900*. Cranbury, N.J.: A.S. Barnes, 1957.

Wilson, Everett B. *America East: Its Architecture and Decoration*. New York: A.S. Barnes & Co., Inc., 1965.

Yarwood, Doren. *Encyclopedia of Architecture*. New York: Facts On File Publications, 1986.

Periodicals

Goyne, Nancy A. "American Windsor Chairs: A Style Survey." *The Magazine Antiques*, April 1969.

Grant, Ellsworth S. "The Mainstream of New England." *American Heritage*, April 1967.

Kirk, John T. "Sources of Some American Regional Furniture Part I." *The Magazine Antiques*, December 1985.

Kirk, John T. "The Tradition of English Painted Furniture Part I: The Experience in Colonial New England." *The Magazine Antiques*, May 1980.

McCarry, Charles, and Arnold, David L. "Yesterday Lingers Along the Connecticut." *National Geographic Magazine*, September 1972.

Symonds, R.W. "The Evolution of the Cupboard." *Connoisseur*, December 1943.